Cultural
and
Educational
Excellence
Revisited

Knowing, Doing, Being, and Becoming as
Though Saving the African American
Child Matters

Shanna L. Broussard, Rh.D.
J. R. Cummings Ph.D.
James A. Johnson, Jr., Ph.D.
Krista A. Levi, M. Ed
and
M. Danita Bailey-Perry, Ph.D.

Portland • Oregon

www.inkwaterpress.com

Paperback ISBN 1-59299-136-X
Hardback ISBN 1-59299-137-8

Publisher: Inkwater Press

Printed in the U.S.A.

ACKNOWLEDGEMENTS

We would like to acknowledge all of our family and friends who supported and encouraged us in the writing of this book. We would especially like to acknowledge our loved ones Victoria, Shari L., and Cornelius, for their love and patience and our ancestors who have been our inspiration and who are featured on the cover of this book. They are:

Savanna and Paul Broussard – parents of Shanna Broussard

Louise Thompson – mother of Jay Cummings

Sam Johnson – grandfather of James Johnson

Kenneth and Lenora Levi – parents of Krista A. Levi

Lillian R. Wynn-Allen – mother of M. Danita Bailey-Perry

A special thanks goes to Mrs. Dora White for the administrative time and assistance she provided us in publishing this book.

TABLE OF CONTENTS

WE is gathahed hyeah, my brothahs,

In dis howlin' wildaness,

Fu' to speak some words of comfo't

To each othah in distress.

An' we chooses fu' ouah subjic'

Dis — we'll 'splain it by an' by;

"An' de Lawd said, ' Moses, Moses,'

An' de man said, 'Hyeah am I.'"

Now ole Pher'oh, down in Egypt,

Was de wuss man evah bo'n,

An' he had de Hebrew chillun

Down dah wukin' in his co'n;

'T well de Lawd got tiahed o' his foolin',

An' sez he: "I'll let him know —

Look hyeah, Moses, go tell Pher'oh

Fu' to let dem chillun go."

An Ante-Bellum Sermon
By Paul Lawrence Dunbar
http://www.plethoreum.org/dunbar/gallery/AnAnte-BellumSermon.asp

Cultural and Educational Excellence Revisited

CHAPTER ONE

INTRODUCTION

The Centurion…commanded that they which could swim should cast them-
selves first into the sea and get to land. And the rest, some on boards and
some on broken pieces of the ship. And so it came to pass, that they escaped
all safe to land.

THE ACTS OF THE APOSTLES, CHAPTER 27

In 1984 the National Alliance of Black School Educators (NABSE) pub-lished a report entitled *Saving the African American Child.* A letter from Dr. Don Smith, who in 1984 was NABSE's sitting president and by whose leadership the report was conceived and developed, prefaced the report with, in part, "*Saving the African American Child,* is a philosophical statement of belief and expectation. It provides the basis for an education whose content is true, appropriate and relevant and whose processes are demo-cratic and humane…. While our single objective is to save African Ameri-can children," Dr. Smith went on, "we believe that all American children will be better served by an educational system which is based on the goals of academic and cultural excellence as defined in this report." The *Saving the African American Child* Report is a vital component of the conceptual framework of this text. The Report provides the foundation on which this book is written in term of providing definitions that underlie and promote its mission and purpose. It is with this in mind that the authors address this book to the broad array of stakeholders who have an interest in and com-mitment to saving the African American child.

Saving the African American Child (1984) offered a set of guidelines to stakeholders who have an interest in and are committed to the education of African American children. *Cultural and Educational Excellence Revisited* suggests that although this interest and commitment has captured the attention of researchers for over two decades, there is a need to take stock and make efforts to understand whether or not things have progressed, regressed or remained the same.

Without a foundation it is difficult at best, or nearly impossible to fully comprehend or understand anything. Therefore, it is important that definitions are extended to our readers as a foundation for *Knowing, Doing, Being and Becoming as though Saving the African American Child Matters.* A solid foundation equals and enables one's understanding and comprehension.

Each of the following definitions presented are done in terms of the African American Learner. Educational Excellence is defined in the *Saving the African American Child* Report, among other phenomena, as "successful efforts of those educational institutions which provide major assistance to African American people in fulfilling needs to alter those elements of the social structure in ways that will promote equal opportunity for all in the society at large" (NABSE, 1984, p. 12). According to the *Saving the African American Child* Report (1984) quality education, "has to do with the *output* of those educational institutions whose policies and practices contribute significantly to the intellectual, physical, and psychological preparation of individuals for effective and satisfying participation in society." *Quality* and *excellence* in education for African Americans include, *Saving The African American Child* goes on, "excellence in the 'basic skills,' in liberal, vocational, economic, political, and spiritual education." Additionally, it includes, "excellence in ridding our people of all vestiges of miseducation" (NABSE, 1984, p. 14). These twin concepts: altering "those elements of the social structure in ways that will promote equal opportunity for all in the society at large," and "ridding our people of all vestiges of miseducation" (NABSE, 1984, p. 7) are closely related to the discussion of cultural excellence found in the *Saving The African American Child* Report.

Cultural Excellence is defined in the report as extents to which the children of a people enjoy a quality of life superior to that of their parents. According to *Saving the African American Child*, a culture is functional "when the group is able to preserve itself, reproduce itself and care for its progeny, when the group's birth rate exceeds its death rate, when the mortality rate of the group is average or normal, and when the progeny are as successful as the parent group. Cultural performance is excellent when the group's birth rate exceeds its death rate, infant mortality is below normal, the mortality rate of the group is superior to the average and the progeny are more successful than the parent group in social progress using education, income, occupation, and political office holders as indicators, and when the group is conscious of its history and culture" (NABSE, 1984, pp. 12-13).

In *Cultural and Educational Excellence Revisited* the authors question the assignment of time and effort to improve the performances of schools serving learners of African descent while ignoring the cultural excellence issue. Of what value is excellent school performance with learners of African descent, we ask, if those learners are to graduate and enter a world not characterized by cultural excellence? *Saving The African American Child* encapsulates this dilemma with: "A quality education experience is dependent upon an adequate basic quality of life" (NABSE, 1984, p. 29) and presents means by which this dilemma may be resolved: "African American educators have a special responsibility to African American children, a responsibility that is over and beyond the work which we already perform. Many of us work in the mainstream and many of us belong to traditional mainstream professional organizations. Yet, our children still have needs that none of these has or will address. To the extent that we can, we must carry an extra load" (NABSE, 1984, p. 34). An aspect of that work involves advancing, in the words of former President Smith, the "philosophical and statement of belief and expectation" upon which the *Saving the African American Child* report rests. Therein lies the purpose of *Cultural and Educational Excellence Revisited*.

Others have contributed in various ways to this purpose. For example, three years after the publication of the *Saving the African American Child* report NABSE published a report titled *"Blueprint for leadership: The Mission - The Model."* This report, referred to as the "progeny of *Saving the African American Child*" by NABSE's 1987 sitting President Dr. Charles Thomas, was "designed to translate the 1984 publication's philosophy and expectations regarding the achievement of academic and cultural excellence into operational terms. *Blueprint* quotes extensively from *Saving the African American*

Child and describes an Educational Development Plan (EDP), essential components of the EDP were a Demonstration School Project (DSP), a NABSE research and Development Institute, and a foundation.

In *Cultural and Educational Excellence Revisited*, the prevailing view of leadership as the capacity to influence behaviors and attitudes in an organizational context is explored against the opportunities for educational and cultural excellence. The view surrounds an expectation that leaders can produce positive results through both their ability and willingness to think critically and solve problems. This view can be examined by inspecting the content, subjects, and knowledge covered in the curriculum of the schools historically. It is evident from the adherence to the "Seven Cardinal Principles" to the content standards and assessment standards of the accountability movement associated closely with federal mandates under the No Child Left Behind Act of 2001 (NCLB). The fundamental understanding of the agreements connected to what children must learn and what teachers must teach is that at its best the items that make the list do not come close to accommodating all there is to know or be able to do. As a matter of fact, it strengthens the assertions about the power of the status quo in crafting educational policies that legitimize the current societal realities for so many people along race and class perspectives.

Although dealing with the paradoxes created by leading an institution such as a school that is promoted as a "great equalizer," educational leaders must often contend with state legislatures that are empowered by their Constitutions to maintain the status quo. Another example occurs when counterproductive policies serve as disincentives for ensuring that students in programs such as Title I and Special Education are successfully exited and returned to the regular classroom. This success is met with a reduction in funding that impacts negatively the services provided by the programs.

To address, adequately, the leadership challenge and the recognition of the importance of academic and culture excellence when building the capacity to transform low achieving schools, the NABSE embarked in 1988 on the Demonstration Schools/ Communities Initiative. The primary mission of the initiative is to identify effective schools that are guaranteeing a quality education to African American students from low income communities. The criteria and standards were defined in *Saving the African American Child* and *The Blueprint for Leadership*, and operationalized through the initiative. The four criteria are delineated as follows:

1) The percentage of the enrollment of the candidate school accounted for by learners of African descent is at least 20 percent greater than the percentage of the state enrollment accounted for by learners of African descent.

2) A state or local NABSE affiliate must provide evidence that the affiliate has involved the candidate school's principal, teachers, other school staff, parents, community leaders and other partners collaborating with the candidate school in at least one successful joint initiative in the last two years. The joint initiatives must have been designed to result in improved results of schooling for learners of African descent.

3) The school/community has demonstrated an interest in increasing achievement levels of learners of African descent in reading, mathematics, communications, critical thinking, and problem solving and in developing exemplary character and good citizenship.

4) The school/community has provided evidence that a strengths and opportunities needs assessment has been conducted in concert with the nominating NABSE affiliate, the local school district, and the local school/community.

In addition to these criteria, Task Force III outlined nine standards that must be met to qualify a school for the Initiative. The standards are:

- Effective Leadership
- Mission Statement
- Maximum Performance Expectations for Students and Staff
- Cultural Excellence
- Relevant and Effective Curricula
- Student Progress Monitoring and Reporting
- Safe, Positive Climate
- Active Parent/Community Participation
- Civic Responsibility and Participation" (Task Force III, 2001).

As a consequence of the vision and dedication of Task Forces I and II, NABSE, Task Force III has selected 17 schools over a five-year period to join the Initiative. The schools were successful in navigating a rigorous process that included identification, nomination, application, desk audit, site validation, and approval by the Executive Board of NABSE. These schools serve as exemplary models for educational leaders who exhibit the passion and commitment needed to know, do, be, and become necessary, successful and effective. "The schools and communities are acknowledged because of newsworthy and notable achievements in places where there are no shortages of individual, collective and institutional challenges" (Task Force III, 2003). Cummings (2003) indicated that "It is against this backdrop of achievement where our schools negate the concepts of 'learned hopelessness' and 'learned helplessness' that NABSE envisioned how important the initiative would be to the membership, leadership and the enterprise of schooling that must deliver quality, equity, and efficiency for the students we are privileged to serve" (Task Force III, 2003). These educational leadership factors and characteristics are vital to the revisiting of cultural and educational excellence in the chapters that follow.

Educational excellence begins with stakeholder leadership. Stakeholder leadership begins with the evolution of events, cases, or other observations, which dictate and contribute to the growth of a movement. Subsequently, the educational characteristics which arise as a result of these events or cases promote change.

In 1995 Coleman filed a legal brief In The United States District Court For The Western District Of Missouri (Western Division) titled "Brief of the Kansas City Citizens for Quality Education, Respecting Remedy, as Amicus Curiae." The brief's focus was a "remedy for disestablishing the vestiges of the dual system of state-imposed segregation found to be extant in the Kansas City, Missouri School District." In the brief Coleman quotes extensively from *Saving the African American Child,* citing NABSE with "The National Alliance of Black School Educators, Incorporated's Task Force on Black Academic and Cultural Excellence issued a seminal report in November 1984 entitled *Saving the African-American Child.*" Coleman goes on to quote from the *Saving the African American Child* Report sharing that the "ethos" of the report [may be the found in the statement:]

NABSE Demonstration Schools/Communities Initiative

Phase I (1998)

1. Thurgood Marshall Elementary School
Seattle Public Schools
Seattle, Washington

2. Hilliard Elementary School
North Forest Independent School District
Houston, Texas

3. Sagamore Hills Elementary School
Fort Worth Independent School District
Fort Worth, Texas

4. Jefferson Elementary School
Gary School Corporation
Gary, Indiana

5. Horace Mann High School
Gary School Corporation
Gary, Indiana

6. Lincoln Humanities Maguet High School
Dallas Independent School District
Dallas, Texas

Phase II (1999)

7. H.O. Burgess Elementary School
Atlanta Public Schools
Atlanta, Georgia

8. George P. Goodale Elementary School
Detroit Public Schools
Detroit, Michigan

9. Green Bay Elementary School
North Chicago Public Schools
North Chicago, Illinois

10. Byron Kilbourn Elementary School
Milwaukee Public Schools
Milwaukee, Wisconsin

11. Lara B. Peck Elementary School
Houston Independent School District
Houston, Texas

Phase III (2001)

12. Joseph J. Rhoads Elementary School
Dallas Independent School District
Dallas, Texas

13. Ronald Edmonds Learning Center
Middle School 113
New York Public Schools
Brooklyn, New York

Phase IV (2002)

14. Rosa Lee Easter Elementary School
Houston, Independent School District
Houston, Texas

15. Julia C. Frazier Elementary School
Dallas Independent School District
Dallas, Texas

Phase V (2003)

16. Cass Technical High School
Detroit Public Schools
Detroit, Michigan

17. Samuel W. Mason Elementary School
Boston Public Schools
Boston, Massachusetts

"'Excellence' in education is much more than a matter of high test scores on standardized minimum or advanced competency examinations. We expect the schools to expand the scope of knowledge and to develop the rational reflective and critical capacities of our children. We have every right to expect that, upon completion of public school work, our children will have the general skills to enter the world of work and to be fully functional members of the society. But more than this, we want the *content* of education to be *true*, *appropriate*, and *relevant*. We want the educational *processes* to be *democratic* and *humane*. We want the *aim* of educational processes to be the complete development of the person and not merely preparation for the available low-level jobs, or even for high-level jobs, that may serve no purpose beyond individual enhancement.

(NABSE, 1984, p. 15)

Among other things," the brief continues, "excellence in education must prepare a student for *self-knowledge* and to become a contributing problem-solving member of his or her own community and in the wider world as well. No child can be ignorant of or lack respect for his or her own unique cultural group and meet others in the world on an equal footing. We believe that this type of excellence in education is a right of the masses and is not merely for a small elite." (NABSE, 1984, p.11)

Dr. Asa Hilliard (1998) in a paper titled "The Standards Movement: Quality Control or Decoy?" raises the following question: "Is the standards movement a quality control movement, as it is advertised, or is it a decoy for something else?" Dr. Hilliard citing *Saving the African American Child* as his source goes on to state the following: "Let me say at the outset that no one fears high standards, at least no Africans that I know. We do not fear clear standards. We do not fear uniform standards. We do not fear public standards. In fact, we have been at the forefront of standards of the highest order." The standards to which Dr. Hilliard refers are reproduced, fully, in Chapter III.

Two years later Dr. Hilliard published a paper titled "Excellence In Education Versus High-Stakes Standardized Testing" in the *Journal Of Teacher Education* (Hilliard, 2000). In this paper he not only cites the previously referenced high standards called for in *Saving the African American Child*, he also cites general academic goals which transcend the disciplines specific to the high standards called for in *Saving the African American Child*, including the demonstration of critical thinking, the demonstration of creativity, the acquisition of a systematic approach to problem solving, and the demonstration of an understanding of the scientific method.

Additionally, *Saving the African American Child* has been placed on numerous reading lists and bibliographies including *Education Reforms and Students at Risk: A Review of the Current State of the Art* dated January 1994; a 1993 African-American Bibliography from the University Of Pennsylvania –African Studies Center; and a 1993 African-American Bibliography from the University of the State of New York.

As we continue to study and develop plausible explanations for the academic and cultural performances of institutions that purport to serve African Americans that will impact the quest for educational and cultural excellence, we must give considerable thought and review to the need for a more substantive understanding of … phenomena that directly influence the nature of these performances. One cannot develop appropriate models for the delivery of service nor can one make necessary decisions for change and for the preparation and development of quality educational programs, if one does not continuously examine ones condition and oneself.

Saving The African American Child describes some of the important social, economic and educational conditions that impact the cultural performance of Americans of African decent. In the quest to thoroughly examine these phenomena, various indicators of social progress were reviewed over a period of time. The National Alliance of Black School Educators' report quotes Weinberg (1977), "For African Americans as a group, 'Equity and Equality are illusions today just as they have always been throughout the history of the Nation'" (NABSE, 1984, p.16). The NABSE report continues this discussion by reminding us that many of the promises and expectations of African Americans have not come to pass. For example, even though the Constitution of the United States promises equal protection under the law, equity in treatment has not yet come.

That even though the dream has always been there, the general economic level of African Americans has always been proportionately lower than that of white Americans. Even though there has been support for social programs over the years, racism and discrimination are still prevalent in this country. Perhaps the effects of racism and discrimination within this country have contaminated almost every facet of society as we experience it and live it today. Specifically, above all and foremost we can easily observe the gap in outcomes of schooling for learners of African descent versus the children and youth of others.

The authors of *Saving The African American Child* discussed the significance of housing, health care, nutrition, employment and other social indicators to the enhancement of the teaching and learning process. The NABSE report indicated that *"A quality educational experience is dependent upon an adequate basic quality of life"* (NABSE, 1984, p.13). In *Cultural and Educational Excellence Revisited*, the authors have taken a renewed look at these same indicators of social progress and how these indicators have impacted the cultural performances of African Americans historically and presently. The existence of these various factors significantly influence whether or not a child has a successful school and/or family life experience. Especially since our schools are usually only a reflection of the society in which we live.

The authors are university professors deeply committed to providing better school performance with results of schooling for African American learners. This commitment is a creature of their diverse backgrounds, training and experience; beliefs, values and attitudes or expectations; and concerns regarding the conditions, practices and results of schooling for African American learners. They have quoted copiously from the *Saving the African American Child* document. Dr. Cummings previously served as President of the Texas Alliance of Black School Educators (TABSE), the Texas affiliate of NABSE, and is in his sixth year as Chairman of NABSE's twenty-three member National Demonstration Schools/Communities Taskforce. Dr. Johnson is a co-author of *Saving the African American Child*. In this Chapter we contribute to the realization of NABSE's Mission as articulated in the *Saving the African American Child* report.

While this is not to give the impression that we must develop a "victim," mentality, it does however mean that we must be knowledgeable of the barriers that impact school and family life and we must develop models and systems to address them and offer solutions to these various barriers.

Without the continuous evaluation of the status and performance of African Americans within the context of these social problems and institutions, and without acknowledging the contribution of these social indicators to the school and life experience of a child, we will not achieve our goal of cultural and academic excellence. *Academic excellence cannot be reached without cultural excellence.* (NABSE, 1984, p.23) Without question, the most ideal situation would be one where the academic environment and the social environment are mutually supportive of the growth and achievement of our children, we must affirm Ron Edmonds premise that:

> "The educability of students derives far more from the nature of the school in which they are sent than it derives from the nature of the family from which they come."
>
> (Edmonds, 1981)

Knowledge for stakeholders who have an interest in and commitment to the education of African American children is essential within the context of *Saving the African American Child*. It is also vital as a change agent. Several issues related to knowledge for stakeholders have a profound impact on the issue at hand.

Issues associated with quality, equity and efficiency as described in *Saving the African American Child* (Task Force on Black Academic and Cultural Excellence, 1984) under topics on Educational Excellence, Cultural Excellence and Leadership can be connected from the 1896 Plessy case to the 1954 Brown case to the current debate related to the efficacy of the the the implementation of the *No Child Left Behind Act of 2001* (NCLB). When one opens the lens on each of the topics, it becomes clear that while much has been examined and proposed, the practices and policies remain the same essentially. This predicament is not unusual in the often emotion-laden school reform environment where the status quo can be a powerful advocate or adversary or both. It is against this backdrop of the illusion of change that the proponents of the status quo have chosen to create false hopes and questionable practices.

Schmoker (2004) suggested as much when pointing to the failure of popular reform and improvement models "as unnecessary complex reforms that have had only the most negligible impact on what should be our core concern: the quality of teaching students receive" (Schmoker, 2004). For example, despite court decisions, staff developments, and effective affirmative action programs, the positive attitudes and behaviors that champion cultural diversity as a strength are heard rarely in the current policy environment. This is an environment that has been reduced to developing and implementing redistributive as opposed to distributive educational policies. Rather than supporting through resources the development of data driven and results based research, the strategy has been to fund only programs that are data driven and results based. On the face of this dilemma must rest the often-noted dearth of data driven, results-based research in the field of education. It is precisely these policy flip-flops that keep the school reform agenda in disarray.

Our task would not be complete or whole without a careful examination of education in an historical context. For it is within this search and examination of various prior events that we frame the current text. Through our search for knowledge, possible explanations, or theories related to the African American Child, we will begin with the recent history of the education of African Americans. Over fifty years ago, the fight began. And here, fifty years later, the fight continues.

What may be discovered in this treatise is that history does, in fact, repeat itself. When this occurs, the reader will be able to contemplate the strength of the statement "the more things change, the more they remain the same" and thusly confirm the power of the status quo. The descriptive framework will feature an examination of the factors and dispositions that existed prior to the 1954 Brown decision and connect the degree of progress to the environment 50 years later.

Concerns about quality programs and access to effective schools by the African American community provided the foundation for the principles argued in the Brown v. Topeka Board of Education case. The strategies employed by the plaintiffs included a display of the psychological damage that segregation had on African American children and was illustrated by Dr. Kenneth Clark in the Black and white dolls comparison. Thus the decision held high expectations for the African American community inclusive of quality, equity, access and integration. These expectations encountered the resistance of the privileged class who were vested in maintaining a status quo that reap educational benefits on their children based on race and socio-economic status.

Some analyses of the current environment surrounding the Brown decision are stating that the concerns about race have shifted to poverty. While there is some movement in this direction with the school finance equity discussions, the overriding evidence supports the fact that race and ethnicity are still significant.

While this statement should not be misconstrued as the relegation of resources and access to the back burner, it may be a stronger fact that the cycle of poverty was viewed as a means to justify the continuation of the "separate, but equal" clause that had resulted in discrimination based on race and ethnicity as ends. The policy environment where these debates are highly contested and combustible often confuses subtle references to distinctions between means and ends as insignificant. At the base of the controversy might be how the status quo grants privilege according to race, gender, ethnicity, and wealth.

An historical perspective and various aspects of educational leadership characteristics have been discussed. So the question becomes now that we have ascertained certain information, what do we do with it? Logically speaking, we should provide a linkage between the information we know with common practices, or with what we do.

In returning to linkages of past and present actions, the linkages between leadership and cultural as well as academic excellence must be addressed. For example, the present school reform climate includes a planning process, often referred to as tactical or strategic, that involves a broad spectrum of stakeholders in the process so that vision, mission and belief statements are developed that serve to define the district, school, or classroom.

The leadership challenge and opportunity discussed in the National Alliance of Black School Educators (NABSE) publication *Saving the African American Child* was amplified further in the delineation of Ron Edmonds' characteristics of effective schools research. Implicit for leaders who are practicing educators and explicit to those aspiring educators is a quote from the NABSE report which follows:

"Contrary to some professional thinking, the capacity of African American children to learn is intact, in spite of the malignant neglect by our social, educational and other systems. The major problems are the problem of resources and the problem with the national, state, and local will and commitment to insure our children's needs are met."

(Task Force on Black Academic and Cultural Excellence, 1984)

This problem statement captures the essence of the leadership challenge that has existed and persisted from the 1954 Brown case and beyond to the resource hampered national policy implementation of NCLB. Another assertion from the NABSE report goes to the heart of complicity by established institutions whose policies have been developed and implemented to protect and preserve the status quo.

"One of the central problems that blocks the attainment of African American academic and cultural excellence is the legacy of racism or the belief in White supremacy and superiority and its concomitant imputation of inferiority. African Americans seek equal access to educational opportunity and redress for prior deprivations caused by slavery, segregation, racism, and poverty."

(Task Force on Black Academic and Cultural Excellence, 1984)

When we view the present climate in the country with the re-emergence of hate groups, blatant attacks on Affirmative Action Programs, and court decisions that accommodate conservative ideologies, rather than judicial activism, it should be crystal clear that much remains to be done throughout the society. This is particularly true of the so-called great equalizer commonly referred to as a "quality education." Some African Americans have championed the Reparations Movement as more of them attempt to have the larger society address and redress the continuing negative vestiges of a society steeped in providing privilege for Whites, while continuing to deny their complicity for the plight of some African Americans and their families.

These are the conditions and issues that can be traced from the "Separate, but Equal Doctrine" articulated in the Plessy case, the precedent setting result of the Brown case, and the recent decisions in Gratz v. Bollinger (Gratz v. Bollinger, 539 U.S. 244, 2003) and (Grutter v. Bollinger,

539 U.S. 306, 2003) the University of Michigan Supreme Court Cases that gave mixed messages to proponents and opponents of Affirmative Action alike. What seems to be obvious is that the central problem discussed in the NABSE report is connected through the Brown Case's clause of "With All Deliberate Speed" regarding implementation of the Standards-based School Reform promises of equity, excellence, and efficiency.

Not withstanding the conditions of past or current state of educational institutions, and regardless of the numerous attempts to effect educational excellence, we all must continually strive to enhance the African American child's experience within the educational institution. Our continued dedication to improving the African American Child's experience should ultimately have a positive effect.

In recognition of the reality that historically leadership to the pursuit of educational and cultural excellence has been given by centurions, too numerous to list here, we began this Chapter quoting from Chapter 27 of *The Acts of the Apostles,* where we find a Centurion managing diverse strengths and abilities among those in his command in such a way that "it came to pass, that they escaped all safe to land." The authors trust that readers of *Cultural and Educational Excellence Revisited,* centurions in the systems or sub-systems to which we contribute or exert control – be it homes, communities, educational institutions, religious institutions, and/ or networks - will contribute to this quest to *Save the African American Child* by effecting excellence.

As we discuss this quest for educational and cultural excellence, let us keep in mind that as a result of our experience in what Dunbar referred to as "dis howlin' wildaness" we are not ordinary or typical centurions and that the emphasis on the word "all" in our opening quote, as in "they escaped all safe to land," renders our responsibility to learners of African descent broad and deep. Some insight into this responsibility may be seen in the following comment made by Gayle Gardner, a sports reporter who was quoted in Sports Illustrated in June of 1991(p. 87).

It was so hard to pry this door open, and if I mess up I know the people behind me are going to have it that much harder. Because then there's living proof. They can sit around and say, "See? It doesn't work." I don't want to be their living proof.

For some stakeholders who have an interest in and a commitment to saving the African American child, what follows may be personal. For the "people behind me" may be our own children or grand children – or my own- or yourself. Given the background discussed above and this thought we turn to a short discussion of the structure of *Cultural and Educational Excellence Revisited.*

Chapters II, III and IV depend, greatly, on research papers developed for and read at conferences between 2001 and 2003. While these papers predate the conception of *Cultural and Educational Excellence Revisited,* the embedded concepts continue to be valid. Many of these ideas have been updated as we focus on our twin themes: educational and cultural excellence. In Chapter II we focus on the Cultural Excellence theme by drawing on the works of Drs. Cummings, Johnson and Bailey-Perry with "Cultural Performances of Americans of African Descent: Using Indicators of Social Progress as Measures of Qualities of Life." The authors use the NABSE definition of cultural performance to establish background and context for their work. The NABSE definition states that cultural performance is excellent "…when the group's birth rate exceeds its death rate, infant mortality is below normal, the mortality rate of the group is superior to the average and the progeny are more successful than the parent group in social progress using education, income, occupation and political office holders as indicators…"(NABSE, pp. 12-13). The authors use these same indicators and have, in fact, expanded their list of indicators as the basis for their research.

The intent of Chapter II is to determine extents to which cultural performance is excellent by further reviewing and examining the nature of the various cultural performances of Americans of African descent. Four questions are identified and used to explore this phenomenon. These questions are:

1. What are some of the facts and characteristics associated with cultural performances of Americans of African decent?
2. How do the cultural performances of Americans of African descent compare with the cultural performances of Americans of non-African decent?
3. Given the NABSE definition of excellent cultural performance,

to what extent may the cultural performances of African American citizens be judged as excellent?

4. What steps or actions can be taken that will improve the cultural performances of Americans of African decent?

These four research questions are examined by using education, elected politicians, employment, health, homeownership, income, longevity and wealth as indicators of social progress. Literature reviews, recent statistics, reports, conditions, expert opinions and various other sources of data served as information sources and proved useful in this study. After probing cultural performance using these indicators, the authors attempt to further explain the context of the outcomes as it relates to the interaction of African Americans with the American social system and the larger external environment. By viewing schools as an educational social system, and operating out of the assumptions that social systems are open and involve people who behave based on their needs and roles, one can then interpret what occurs between individuals and the larger environment and use this to predict the dynamics that might forecast and explain the cultural performance of African Americans. The authors surmise in Chapter II that various groups and entities in an individual's life impact that individual's performance and the performance of the group to which the individual belongs. The success or failure of this life cycle, along with these experiences, impacts school success and ultimately life-decision choices.

The theme of Chapter III is Educational Excellence. In Chapter III we draw on the work of Drs. Cummings and Johnson with "Necessity plus Possibility: School Performance with Children and Youth of African Descent and Resulting Performance Gap Identification."

Often times, when problems or issues arise, we tend to respond to the problem or react to the problem. A reaction to the problem does not necessarily ensure a successful solution to that problem, or that the problem will be solved or fixed. When responding, we should be cognizant of to what we are responding. Are we responding to the problem or are we responding to the possibilities? When responding to problems, solutions become somewhat limited. While on the other hand, when responding to the possibilities, solutions become unlimited, where there are no boundaries when seeking solutions.

A viable option for educator preparation and in-service programs can be found in the utilization of the J curve which challenges the assumptions of the normal curve. While the normal curve purports that diversity within a population be viewed as weakness, the J curve insists that diversity be viewed as a strength. Indications are that the provision of three factors in a teaching and learning situation proportional to the needs of students can produce academic excellence. These factors are: 1) adequate time; 2) quality teaching; and 3) positive experiences in the classroom and school. Incidentally, these factors are often controlled by the resources allocated to the school and the leadership of the principal or superintendent.

An unpublished 2003 study conducted in Florida and Texas that examined the characteristics needed for effective educational leadership in the years 2005-2040 revealed the following: "1) Technologically literate, 2) Human Relations Skills, 3) Global Awareness, 4) Multi Language Acquisition, 5) Ability to Deal with Change, 6) Lifelong Learner" (Cummings and Wentz, 2003) Responders to the survey agreed that these are the essential characteristics that are needed for effective, efficient, and successful educational leaders during the time frame of 2005-2040.

When these continuing educational leadership factors and characteristics are compared with the difficulties of effecting positive change in status quo institutions such as educational and religious institutions, and governmental entities, it becomes clear that knowledge, skill, determination, perseverance, and passion are part of the equation as well. Once the educational and socialization processes are understood fully by the leadership, then the re-education of those dedicated teachers and other school and district personnel can proceed along the appropriate route of connecting programs and practices to students and communities. Continuing the major theme of this text, cultural and educational excellence, we must seek to recognize where African American children fall within this continuum so that we can offer more accurate solutions to the issue at hand.

The interaction of educational and cultural excellence is the theme of Chapter IV. This theme is approached by drawing on the work of Drs. Broussard and Johnson, and Miss Levi with "The Educational Branding Hypothesis: Branding African American Learners at an Early Age."

How do we want our African American children to be treated within the educational institutions? Fair and equitable treatment is what we expect, but is that what we get? Unfortunately, fair and equitable treatment is not rendered in all cases. In some instances our African American children are being branded at an early age and are subsequently being assigned to certain instructional tracks based on the brand they are given.

In Chapter IV, the authors cite Farmer (2002) who connected this concept of branding to expectations forcefully for consideration by educational leaders:

> "The brand bestowed on a given learner is bestowed by design and is a creature of the coexistence of the vision held for the learner by those who have the power and authority to make a decision about the education of the learner, the culture of the school or the rules and regulations that govern the behavior of school role incumbents such as counselors, teachers and administrators; and how stakeholders think about and value the learner."
>
> (Broussard, Johnson, and Levi, 2003)

Since most educators, through experience and training, are socialized by status quo beliefs and values, leaders must be positioned to challenge traditional practices that result in the sorting of students, and be able to articulate and demand an operational and attitudinal paradigm shift that embraces diversity as a strength. An excellent example of the training bias that reinforces this branding practice is the reliance on the normal or bell-shaped curve to explain variations in human performance and disguise it as variations in human ability. This socialization process is embedded in the prevailing theories and practices of educator preparation programs. It operates on the theoretical base that only certain students can achieve at high academic levels, while others are destined for less demanding options and even career choices. It protects the status quo by ensuring that the "Haves" and "Have Nots" in the society remain in social and economic strata akin to where they are in terms of socio-economic status and racial classification. Educational leadership must recognize that unless there is a major intervention that teaches new ways of thinking and acting, the benefactors of the status quo will unite to squelch any meaningful change.

Finally, the authors feel it incumbent upon themselves to say a word about the methodology at issue in *Cultural and Educational Excellence Revisited.* In 1990 Ernest L. Boyer, President of the Carnegie Foundation for the Advancement of University Teaching, published **Scholarship Reconsidered: Priorities of the Professoriate** arguing that our understanding of scholarship is tantamount to a myopic focus on the discovery of "new knowledge" for its own sake, and that other equally valid and important functions such as teaching and the collation of existing knowledge are driven by, rather than coequal with "research." Boyer proposed in **Scholarship Reconsidered** a model for scholarship that went beyond the pursuit of new knowledge by legitimating four aspects of academic work:

> Surely, scholarship means engaging in original research. But the work of the scholar also means stepping back from one's investigation, looking for connections, building bridges between theory and practice, and communicating one's knowledge effectively to students. Specifically, we conclude that the work of the professoriate might be thought of as having four separate, yet overlapping, functions. These are: the scholarship of *discovery* [the pursuit of knowledge for its own sake, the discovery of new knowledge]; the scholarship of *integration* [collating, making connections and drawing conclusions from discrete facts and findings]; the scholarship of *application* [responsibly applying knowledge to consequential problems]; and the scholarship of *teaching* [professional practice needing constant reflection and review].
>
> (Boyer, 1990, p. 16)

The reader will find that *Cultural and Educational Excellence Revisited* meets the four Boyer expectations. We report results of our investigations. We connect key concepts. We bridge theory and practice. We communicate knowledge. It is within this framework that we trust that stakeholders who have an interest in and commitment to saving the African American child will join us as we examine and articulate cultural and educational excellence issues in the chapters that follow.

CHAPTER TWO

CULTURAL PERFORMANCES OF AMERICANS OF AFRICAN DESCENT

Using Indicators of Social Progress as Measures of Qualities of Life

"This society is not likely to become free of racism, Thus it is necessary for Negroes to free themselves by becoming their idea of what a free people should be."

ELLISON, 1999, P. 356

Derrick Z. Jackson, a Boston Globe columnist, in an outlook piece entitled "Black's sitting down for all the wrong reasons now" points to "several studies" in the *Journal of the American Medical Association* and the *New England Journal of Medicine* that support the contention of the barber played by Cedric the Entertainer in *Barbershop*, the movie: "Now look at us. Now our problem is that we sit down too much. We used to get mad at white folks for calling us lazy and shiftless. Y'all watch so much television, you wouldn't even notice your own funeral" (in Jackson, 2002). Jackson goes on to support the contention of the barber played by Cedric the Entertainer in *Barbershop*, the movie, with the following data:

- o While 31 percent of Americans overall are obese, 50 percent of African American women are obese.
- o While 57 percent of white women are over-weight, 77 percent of African American women are overweight.

o   The rate of overweight African American children is double that of white children.

Jackson allows as to how the barber played by Cedric the Entertainer in *Barbershop* the movie may be "exaggerating a bit" but he allows, "statistics do not lie. If you ask me, the number one reason [B]lack folks have gotten so huge is our addiction to television. Last year," he goes on, "Nielson Media Research and TN Media found that while the television is on in the average American household 54 hours a week, it is on in African American households for 76 hours per week."

Jackson goes on to share the following as well:

o   "An astounding 42 percent of African American fourth graders watch six or more hours of television a day. That is three times more than the 13 percent of white fourth-graders who watch that much TV and a stunning five times more than Asian/ Pacific Islander fourth –graders."

o   "While only 6 percent of the best readers in the National Assessment of Education Progress tests watch six or more hours of TV a day, 34 percent of poor readers watch that much."

o   A study in North Carolina found that students who watched six or more hours of TV a day were behind a full year or more in their studies. That study found that 40 percent of African American children watched six or more hours, compared with 16 percent of white and Asian-American children.

While it is not our purpose to make real or imagined correlations among ones weight, television watching habits, and academic achievement the focus of this chapter, Jackson's observations are especially instructive, in view of the National Alliance of Black School Educators' (NABSE) definition of culture and survival. Culture is defined by NABSE as "the sum total of artifacts which accumulate as a people struggle for survival and self determination." Survival is defined as "…the preservation of one's people and one's self, the reproduction of one's people and one's self, and the care of the progeny which result" (NABSE, 1984, p. 22).

Jackson's remarks are equally instructive when viewed in the context of NABSE's definition of a functional culture: "a culture is functional when the group is able to preserve itself, reproduce itself, and care for its progeny, when the group's birth rate exceeds its death rate, when the mortality rate of the group is average or normal, and when the progeny are as successful as the parent group. Cultural performance is excellent," the NABSE document goes on, "…when the group's birth rate exceeds its death rate, infant mortality is below normal, the mortality rate of the group is superior to the average and the progeny are more successful than the parent group in social progress using education, income, occupation, and political office holders as indicators, and when the group is conscious of its history and culture" (NABSE, pp. 12-13). Finally, Jackson's observations are instructive because they suggest a need to better understand the nature of the various cultural performances of Americans of African descent.

The purpose of this chapter is to contribute to that better understanding by answering the following questions:

Question I: What are some facts and characteristics associated with cultural performances of Americans of African descent?

Question II: How do the cultural performances of Americans of African descent compare with the cultural performances of Americans of non-African descent?

Question III: Given the NABSE definition of excellent cultural performance, to what extent may the cultural performances of African American citizens be judged as excellent?

Question IV: What steps or actions can be taken that will improve the cultural performances of Americans of African descent?

Our first two questions are: How do the cultural performances of Americans of African descent compare with the cultural performances of Americans of non-African descent, and given the NABSE definition of excellent cultural performance, to what extent may the cultural performances of African American citizens be judged as excellent? These two questions suggest a third question as to how one construes relationships among cultural performances of a people and quality of life outcomes.

It is important to place cultural excellence in the context of curricula goals and methods valued and pursued by school officials and in the context of short and long-range outcomes of schooling for African American versus white children and youth, their families and their communities prior to addressing these questions. A first issue is driven by *excellence*. From the perspective of all taxpayers the value of what is learned in school must be judged in terms of extents to which learner mastery of expected outcomes of schooling result in excellent cultural performances. From the perspective of taxpayers of African descent, the value of what is learned in school must be judged in terms of extents to which there are no significant differences between African American and white learner outcomes of schooling—the *equity* issue.

An underlying and perhaps more significant issue may be inferred from Ralph Ellison's novel, *Juneteenth*. That issue may be stated as follows: Were Americans of African descent, in fact emancipated, or was the emancipation of African Americans an illusion? This question has meaning as, by and large, African and white Americans are born as a result of identical methodologies but, as will be seen below, effect dissimilar cultural performances. Ellison seems to have captured this thought with: "...in this lonely, lightning-bug flash of time we call our life on earth we all begin with a slap of a hand across our tender baby bottoms to start us crying the puzzled question with our first drawn breath: Why was I born?...Aaaaaaaah!" (Ellison, 1999, p. 152). By examining the following set of indicators of social progress: education, elected politicians, employment, health, homeownership, incarceration, income, longevity, and wealth, we shall approach the four previously stated research questions.

EDUCATION AS AN INDICATOR OF SOCIAL PROGRESS

First, let us look at the contribution African American learners have made to school populations in recent years. Extents to which African American learners have contributed to school populations versus extents to which they were suspended or expelled, stated as percentages by school districts and extents to which African American learners contributed to school populations versus the extents to which they were represented in Advanced Placement and "Gifted" programs, stated as percentages by school districts in 1999 are displayed in Tables I and II, respectively.

TABLE I

School districts by percent African American contribution to enrollment and suspensions or expulsions

School Districts	Percent Enrollment	Percent Suspended or Expelled
Austin, Texas	18	36
Boston, Massachusetts	55	70
Chicago, Illinois	53	63
Columbia, South Carolina	78	90
Denver, Colorado	21	36
Durham, North Carolina	58	79
Los Angeles, California	14	30
Miami-Dade County, Florida	33	48
Providence, Rhode Island	23	39
Salem, Oregon	01	04
San Francisco, California	18	56

(Gordon, et al 1999)

TABLE II

School districts by percent African American contribution to enrollment and Advanced Placement and Gifted Programs

School Districts	Percent Enrollment	Percent Advd Place and "Gifted"
Austin, Texas	18	11
Boston, Massachusetts	55	27
Denver, Colorado	21	18
Durham North Carolina	58	26
Los Angeles, California	14	08
Miami-Dade County, Florida	33	23
Providence, Rhode Island	23	09
San Francisco, California	18	05

(Gordon, et al 1999)

Again in 1999, the extents to which African American learners contributed to school populations versus the extents to which African American teachers were represented in the teaching corps, stated as percentages by school districts are displayed in Table III.

These statistics clearly point out that the African American rate of suspension and expulsion from school is significantly higher than African American representation in the total school population, while African American students are significantly underrepresented in Advanced Placement and Gifted programs and in the percentages of African American teachers in the teaching corps of some of the major school districts in the country.

TABLE III

School districts by percent African American contribution to enrollment and Percent of African American Teachers

School Districts	Percent Enrollment	Percent A. A. Teachers
Austin, Texas	18	09
Boston, Massachusetts	55	26
Chicago, Illinois	53	43
Miami-Dade County, Florida	33	28
Denver, Colorado	21	08
Durham, North Carolina	58	32
Los Angeles, California	14	15
Providence, Rhode Island	23	10
Columbia South Carolina	78	40
Salem, Oregon	01	01
San Francisco, California	18	11

(Gordon, et al 1999)

It is pointed out that 37.2 percent of Americans of African descent and 42.4 percent of whites ages 18-24 are enrolled in college. While this gap in enrollment is disconcerting, it is more disconcerting to note that during the period 1997-2000, 20.6 percent of African American high school graduates between the ages 25 of 29 had earned at least a bachelor's degree by 2001 (14.6 percent in Texas – a gap of six points). This was the case for 36.5 percent of comparable whites (32.5 percent in Texas – a gap of four points) (Nissimov, 2002).

Between 1992 and 2001 African American enrollment decreased by 7.9

percent at Texas A & M University and decreased by 12.2 percent at The University of Texas flagship campus in Austin (Rodriquez, 2002). Villafranca (2002) reports that according to the 2000 Census, while African Americans and whites contributed 11.6 and 53.1 percents, respectively, to the population in Texas, they contributed 3.5 percent (African American) and 62.7 percent (white) to the University of Texas at Austin; and 2.4 percent (African American) and 82.0 percent (white) to the Texas A & M enrollments. Further, he reports "from 1991 to 2001, the percentage of African American students dropped to 2.4 from 3 percent."

In some states, the decrease in or failure to increase college attendance of students of African descent may be related to the failure of merit-based state scholarships to meet intended goals. In Georgia, the Helping Outstanding Pupils Educationally program (HOPE) "appears to have benefited white students more than [B]lack youngsters. Compared with nearby states, college attendance among white students in Georgia rose 12.4 percent faster from 1993 to 1997, but remained virtually unchanged for [B]lack students."

In Michigan, Blacks, "who make up about 14 percent of the state's student population, received about 3.5 percent of the money awarded in 1999" from the "two year-old Merit Award Scholarship Program funded with money from the federal tobacco settlement" [The program awards] five one-time grants of $2,500 to students who stay in-state, and $1,000 to students who go out of state.

In Florida, "whites made up 61 percent of students in 1998 but were 77 percent of aid recipients. [B]lacks made up almost 28 percent of students and received about 8 percent of aid" from "Florida's lottery-funded Bright Futures program" (Emery, 2002).

African American students scored lower on the ACT (17) in school year 2001 than they did the previous year (17.1). White students scored higher in school year 2001 (21.6) than they did the previous year (20.1) (Associate Press, 2002). Additionally, while the number of minority students taking the SAT has increased, a gap between the performance of minority and white students continues to persist. Gaps in the performance of ethnic groups also continued to persist on the ACT. In a 2001 report, the average score for white students was 21.8, for African Americans 16.9, for Mexican Americans 18.5 and for American Indians, 18.8. According to

Gaston Caperton, president of the College Board, "these differences illustrate persistent social problems in our country: inequitable access to high-quality education" (Hoover, 2001).

These findings must be considered in light of the fact that, according to an Intercultural Development Research Association (IDRA) report, 46 percent of African American students either drop out or are pushed out of school. The report indicates that IDRA has "conducted an annual attrition study since 1986 to track the number and percent of students in Texas who are lost from public school enrollment prior to graduation." According to the report's preliminary results "following a 16 –year trend, …African American students [had a] 46 percent [attrition rate]…white students had an attrition rate of 26 percent" (Montecel, 2002).

In Arizona, attrition rates for African American versus white students were 32.5% and 24.2%, respectively (Cortez, 2002.) While 43 percent of whites enroll in college after high school this is only the case for 39.4 percent of Blacks. The gap between the college completion rates for white versus African American individuals over the age of 25 has widened (See Table IV). For example, while it was 3.6 percent in 1940, it was 11.5 percent in 2000 (Cole, 2002). According to an Education Trust report, "Of the 772 four –year schools with student bodies that are at least 5 percent Black, nearly 40 percent graduated fewer than 30 percent of their Black students. Sixty-eight schools, or nearly 10 percent, graduated fewer than 10 percent" (Unknown, 2004).

These data describe conditions that become more evident when we zero in on Black graduation rates for football players. The NCAA (2002) reported that "Graduation rates for white football players had jumped from 56 percent to 62 percent in Division I-A between the '94-95 and '96-97 school years, while rates for [B]lack football players had gone from 43 percent to 45 percent." It will be interesting to view what happens to these rates when the class of 2007 graduates. In August of 2003, football players will be admitted under the "New NCAA Academic Reform" – requiring SAT scores as low as 400 (Houston Chronicle, 2003).

TABLE IV

College completion rates for white v. African Americans over the age of 25

	2000	1990	1980	1970	1940
Whites	28.1	22	17.8	11.6	4.9
African American	16.6	11.3	7.9	4.5	1.3
Difference:	11.5	10.7	9.9	7.1	3.6

We cannot discuss education without considering the impact technology has had on our schools. Even though considerable effort has been made to provide Internet access and computers in schools, the same level of access is not always available in the homes of students. The difference is especially apparent in the homes of African American and Hispanic students. According to a 2002 statewide report on technology and readiness in Texas, while many students have access to computers and technology at home, African American and Hispanic students have less access than do white and Asian students (Zuniga, 2003). This, of course, impacts a student's ability to compete in the workplace and in the future. Zuniga reported that only 28% of African Americans and 27% of Hispanics did homework on computers, while 58% of whites did so. This was directly tied to income. Thirty-one percent of students with a family income less than $20,000 used computers at home, while 80% of students with a family income of more than $75,000 had computers (Zuniga, 2003).

ELECTED AFRICAN AMERICAN POLITICIANS AS AN INDICATOR OF SOCIAL PROGRESS

Political power is critical to the advancement of any group. It provides the means through which social injustices can be addressed and by which laws can be established and enforced that affect all Americans, especially African Americans. Clearly, ethnic minorities are under-represented in politics. Kong (2002) cited the National Urban League in its annual report on the *State of Black America*, which reported that "there were more than 9,000 [B]lack elected officials in the year 2000 – more than at any other time in the nation's history." Several decades after the civil rights movement, the number of African American elected politicians is shrinking. This is most noticeable in California.

In the late 1970's things were looking good for African Americans in California politics. In 2000, Oakland, a city in which African Americans make up over 41 % of the overall population, elected its first white mayor in 20 years. Los Angeles' and San Francisco's mayors are also white and [at the time of his report] there [was] not a single African American in state-wide office (Squyres, 2000). Let us remember that California is often the trend-maker for the rest of the nation and note that additional cities previously with African American executives [mayors] such as Houston, Texas, New York City, Chicago, Illinois, Newark, New Jersey, Dayton, Ohio and Columbus, Ohio now have white mayors.

Another significant factor in the drop in the number of African American elected politicians may be attributed to the growth among Hispanic Americans. Fueled by immigration, this population (Hispanic Americans) has doubled and in the 1990's became a major political force.

Bruce Cain, director of the Institute for Governmental Studies at the University of California, Berkeley, explains that many African Americans are moving out of urban centers often into majority white suburbs. In these suburbs they form small minority pockets and seldom run for office. The political result of this redistribution is that African Americans have lost clout in traditional districts and are less politically visible in the new ones (Squyres, 2000).

EMPLOYMENT AS AN INDICATOR OF SOCIAL PROGRESS

One must pause when the participation of Americans of African descent in the labor market is examined. Drawing on material published by the National Urban League in its annual report on the *State of Black America,* Kong (2002) reports that "in June [of 2002] the unemployment rate for whites was 5.2 percent; for [B]lacks it was 10.7 percent." Michael Dyson in his book entitled *I May Not Get There With You* makes significant contributions to our understanding of this category of cultural performances of Americans of African descent. So as to not drown the reader in numbers, the authors have reconfigured Dyson's reporting of percentage distributions of ethnic groups among the various branches of the armed forces in the form of Table V. It may be seen from Table V that: African Americans were over represented in each branch of the armed services. While in 1990 African Americans contributed 12.1 percent to the United States population, they accounted for about 30 percent of the army, 21 percent of the navy, 17 percent of the marines, and 14 percent of the air force. White Americans were under represented in each branch of the armed services. While in 1990 white Americans contributed 81.9 percent to the United States population they accounted for about 65 percent of the Army, 68 percent of the Navy, 73 percent of the Marines, and 81 percent of the Air Force.

TABLE V

Distributions of Ethnic Groups among the Various Branches of the Armed Forces

Branches	Percentage Distributions by Ethnic Groups During Persian Gulf War				
	African American	Latino Minorities	Other Minority	Total	White
Army	29.8	4.2	1.5	35.5	64.5
Navy	21.3	6.0	4.6	31.9	68.1
Marines	16.9	7.9	2.6	27.4	72.6
Air Force	13.5	3.1	2.4	19.0	81.0

While in 1990 African Americans contributed 12.1 percent to the United States population they accounted for about 30 percent of the army, 21 percent of the navy, 17 percent of the marines, and 14 percent of the air force. White Americans were under represented in each branch of the armed services. It may also be seen from Table V that as contributions to the various armed services made by African Americans increase, the contributions of white Americans decrease and vice versus. Percentage comparisons among contributions made by African Americans, Latinos, other minorities, total minorities and whites to the U. S. Population versus the military are found in Table VI.

TABLE VI

Contributions of ethnic groups to the U. S. versus military populations.

Ethnic Groups

	African American	Latino Minorities	Other Minority	Total	White
U. S. Population	12.1	8.3	6.0	26.4	81.9
Military Population	23.0	4.9	4.4	32.0	67.7

Dyson, quoting Derrick Jackson, "summarized the plight of [B]lacks who are vulnerable to the pull of opportunity that military enlistment represents, an indictment of the lack of comparable opportunities in civilian life" with: "Thus, many African –Americans, regardless of income, are so wary of taking out huge college loans that they are easy prey for the military's $2 billion-plus recruiting machine. The promise of free college tuition and free health and life insurance make the so-called diversity efforts of universities and corporations seem impotent. A 1989 National Academy of Sciences report found that 50 percent of African American male seniors and 29 percent of African American female seniors said they had definite or probable plans to enter the military. This compared with 21.3 percent for white male seniors and 5 percent of white female seniors with similar plans."

The "lack of comparable opportunities" claimed by Jackson is supported, in part, again by the Urban Leagues' Annual Report on the *State of Black America* where it is stated that "About 20 percent of [B]lacks hold professional or managerial jobs, while more than 30 percent of whites do." It is also reported that "less than one percent of certified public accountants are [B]lack (Kong, 2002). The dearth of African American head coaches in professional and college football is consistent with Kong's report. According to a November 2002 Associated Press story the National Football League "has two [B]lack coaches among the 32 teams…. [at the college level] of 117 Division I-A football schools only three head coaches are [B]lack….a study conducted by the NCAA showed that 21.2 percent of assistant coaches and 16.6 percent of graduate assistants are [B]lack, and in Division I-AA, there are no [B]lack head coaches when historically [B]lack institutions are excluded….According to NCAA figures, only 25 of 944 athletic directors at non-historically [B]lack colleges identified themselves as [B]lack" (Associated Press, 2002).

It is of interest that unemployment rates for African Americans have consistently been approximately double that of whites (See Table VII) (Flynn, 2002). It is also the case that African Americans on an average earn less than white American counterparts with the same qualifications. Black men who have finished college earn 80 percent of what their white counterparts do, while Black men who have had some college earn 83 percent of what similar whites do. Cole (2002) made the following observation in this regard: "A disproportionate number of minorities continue to live below the poverty level and College-educated African Americans continue to earn less than their Anglo counterparts despite having commensurate skills and abilities. The aforementioned data lead us to question our educational progress as a society. It appears that more years of schooling are not necessarily correlated with economic independence or improved quality of life for minorities. The 'glowing' educational statistics outlined [above] belie a grave national dilemma and allow society to falsely believe that we are making more educational progress than our ancestors." One case in point: Black male attorneys between the ages of thirty-five and forty-five earn seventy-nine cents on the white male dollar. Moreover, the jobless rate for Black college graduates is over twice as high as the white rate—higher than the disparity between high school graduates (Chideya, 1995).

TABLE VII

African American versus white unemployment rates for selected years.

Populations	Selected years				
	1975	1982	1992	2000	2001
African Americans	14.8	18.9	14.2	7.6	8.7
Whites	7.8	8.6	6.6	3.5	4.2

For many years African Americans have experienced race bias in hiring. Some would lead us to believe that discriminatory hiring practices no longer exist, but several experiments give rise to very different conclusions. The September 4, 2003 *Wall Street Journal* reported on experiments conducted in Milwaukee, Chicago, and Boston where young Black and white job applicants with similar job histories and demeanors applied in person for jobs. In the Milwaukee experiment, college graduates who posed as job applicants visited 350 employers. The white applicant was called back 17% of the time, while the Black applicant was called back 14% of the time. In a similar experiment an economist from the Massachusetts Institute of Technology found that using a white sounding name on an application was worth as much as an extra eight years of work experience. Applicants with names like Greg Kelly or Emily Walsh were 50% more likely to get called for interviews than those named Jamal Jackson or Lakisha Washington, names which are far more common for African Americans (Wessel, 2003). These experiments conclude that color does matter.

HEALTH AS AN INDICATOR OF SOCIAL PROGRESS

Data specific to percentages of obesity, and percentages of over-weight African American women versus white women, and rates of overweight African American children versus white children have been previously cited. However, in a report published by the *Congressional Black Caucus*, the Alzheimer's Association estimates that Alzheimer's disease is between 14 and 100 percent more prevalent among Americans of African descent than among whites. Referred to as "a silent epidemic emerging among Americans of African descent, the report indicates "vascular disease as a trigger for Alzheimer's and suggests that high cholesterol and high blood pressure –both subject to self regulation – as significant risk factors" (Scripps Howard News Service, 2002).

Gavin, in his 1954 testimony to the *Congressional Black Caucus* Health Braintrust, reported that "more than 2.1 million African Americas have diabetes" and that the rate "of diabetes prevalence [is] 160% higher in African Americans than the general U. S. population." Gavin also reported that diabetes is "the common denominator" among "kidney disease, heart disease, stroke, blindness, and amputations, …all complications of diabetes." Going on, he indicated that "people with diabetes account for nearly 1/3 of all cases of end-stage renal disease and African Americans with diabetes are 4 times more likely to develop end-stage renal disease than white Americans with diabetes" (Gavin, 1995).

Regarding heart disease, Gavin (1995) reports "in 1990…more than 35,000 African Americans died from heart disease". Additionally, while the death rate for heart disease in African American males was just 1.3% higher than for white males, the death rate for African American females was nearly 30 % higher than white females." In that same year, again according to Gavin, "nearly 15,000 African Americans died from stroke. The death rate for stroke in African American males was 102.5 % higher than for white males and the death rate for females was 79.8% higher than white females." Gavin allows as to how "more than 135,000 African Americans are blind. A recent study" he goes on, "found that African Americans are 3 times more likely to go blind than white Americans" (Gavin, 1995).

"Five studies involving lung cancer found that African Americans were less likely to receive any treatment – even when treated were less likely to have surgery…Six of 23 studies on breast cancer showed substantial variations in how patients were treated, with African Americans being less likely to receive standard radiation therapy after breast-conservation surgery (Jones, 2002).

Further, the following is found in Chapter 2 of a 1999 United States Commission on Civil Rights report entitled *The Role Of Government And Private Health Care Programs And Initiatives, The Health Care Challenge: Acknowledging Disparity, Confronting Discrimination, And Ensuring Equality:*

o   Diabetes rates are 70 percent higher for [B]lacks than for whites.
o   Black children are three times more likely than white children to be hospitalized for asthma."
o   The ratio of AIDS cases to the population for [B]lack men is almost seven times that of white men.
o   [T]here also are great differences in birth weights and infant mortality rates. Blacks have the highest prevalence of low-birth weights of all racial and ethnic categories. In 1995, 13.1 percent of African American babies had a low birth weight, which is defined as weighing less than 5.5 pounds. The infant mortality rate was 14.6 [per 1,000 births.] Comparable data for white infants were 6.2 percent [low birth weight] and 6.3 per 1,000 births [infant mortality rate.]

o In 1996, the death rate, due to breast cancer for African American women, was 26.5 (per 100,000 people), compared with 19.8 for white women. Although the incidence of breast cancer is somewhat lower for African American women compared with white women (100.5 cases per 100,000 and 112.8 cases per 100,000, respectively), African American women are more likely to develop breast cancer at younger ages, and are more likely to die as a result of breast cancer.

According to Giselle Corbie-Smith (University of North Carolina at Chapel Hill) "nearly 80 % of [B]lacks and 52% of whites believe they could be used as 'guinea pigs' for medical research." The study also found that "nearly 42 % of [B]lacks and more than 23% of whites did not trust their doctor to fully explain research participation to them, more than 37% of [B]lacks and nearly 20% of whites thought their doctor might ask them to join a research study –even if it meant they might suffer some harm from an experimental drug, and about 15 % of [B]lacks and 8 % of whites did not feel they could freely question their doctors" (Fakelmann, 2002). Also significant, is that almost" 25% of African Americans and 8% of whites thought their doctors had given them treatment as part of an experiment without their permission" (Fackelmann, 2002). In spite of regulations aimed at protecting human subjects, many Blacks, understandably, remain concerned about being subjected to experiments without their knowledge or consent.

David R. Williams and Chiquita Collins reviewed evidence that led them to suggest that segregation is a primary cause of racial disparities and has been a central determinant for the perpetuation of inequalities for African Americans (Williams, 2001). This is likely to affect the access to and quality of medical care received by members of the African American community. They further identify socioeconomic status as a fundamental cause of inequalities in health, education and employment. In their research they examine *The Economic Report of the President* in 1999. This document, they report, leads them to conclude "…that there was little change in the economic gap between Blacks and whites in the last quarter of the 20th century. In 1978, Black households earned 59 cents for every dollar earned by white households and had a poverty rate that was 3.5 times as high…. In 1996 African American households earned 59 cents in income for every dollar earned by whites, and African Americans had a poverty rate that was 2.5 times as high…. (Williams, 2001). An analysis of these data indicated that a widening in the socioeconomic gap was associated with a widening gap in health.

Recently, researchers have begun to link obesity and related health issues to culture, specifically poverty and low income. In fact, studies have shown that Black neighborhood stores have poor food choices and offer fewer healthful foods than do stores in more affluent neighborhoods (Hellmich, 2003). This makes it more difficult for African Americans to maintain a healthy weight and a healthy lifestyle.

Housing as an indicator of social progress.

Home ownership is the American dream and is clearly an indicator of social progress. It is a dream that cuts across ethnic and geographic boundaries. According to Kong (2002) the National Urban League in its annual report on the *State of Black America* states that "for [B]lacks, the home-ownership rate is 48 percent – the national rate in the 1940s." Ameristat, a publication of the Population Studies Center at the University of Michigan reports that "there are well-documented differences in homeownership rates between whites and other groups. In 2000, about 72 percent of non-Hispanic whites owned homes, compared with…46 percent of African Americans…" Ameristat goes on to report that "for [B]lacks, the difference in homeownership rates was greatest in the Northeast and in the northern Midwest, particularly in North Dakota, where 68 percent of whites owned homes in 2000, but only 18 percent of [B]lacks did' (Ameristat, 2002).

Simmons shares that "compared with their white counterparts, African American households are about 35 percent less likely to own their homes and African American renters are about 20 percent more likely to experience severe housing problems. African Americans are more than 20 times more likely than whites to live in extremely poor city neighborhoods. Such differences in housing outcomes contribute to broader patterns of socioeconomic inequality across population groups" (Simmons, 2000).

An analysis completed by the *Tennessean* of African Americans trying to buy homes in Nashville and surrounding counties, revealed that African

Americans were declined when attempting to borrow money, more often than whites with similar incomes. The *Tennessean* analysis included an analysis of 234,684 loan applications submitted from 1994-2001 in the eight counties of the Nashville metropolitan area. The analysis showed that throughout the eight counties, "African Americans, Hispanics and Native Americans were turned down for mortgage loans more often than whites in the vast majority of cases. The gap tended to widen in upper-income groups" (Wissner, 2003).

The article goes on to reveal the testimony of an expert witness in court cases for minorities who have filed discrimination lawsuits. This expert indicated that often the worst qualified whites get loans when clearly better qualified minorities will be denied loans. He goes on to say that many people just don't make the effort to help out minority applicants but will clearly make suggestions and give breaks to white applicants (Wissner, 2003).

CRIMINAL JUSTICE, INCARCERATION AND PUBLIC SAFETY AS INDICATORS OF SOCIAL PROGRESS.

Salant quoting from a 2002 "government report" points out that in "1990, almost 4.4 million adults" – one in every 32 adults in the United States – "were incarcerated or being supervised." "Whites, according to Salant, accounted for 55 percent of those on probation, while [B]lacks made up 31 percent." However, "46 percent of those incarcerated were [B]lack and [only] 36 percent were white" (Salant, 2002). Relatedly, more than seven out of every ten white New Yorkers rate police protection in the city as good, in comparison to fewer than five of every ten black New Yorkers (Garfinkle, 1999).

Marc Mauer, Assistant Director for the Sentencing Project prepared a report for the U.S. Commission on Civil Rights. In his report, he examines the disproportionate impact of the criminal justice system on the status of the African American male. His report highlights three important facts:

- "Nearly one in three (32%) Black males in the age group 20-29 is under some form of criminal justice supervision on any give day – either in prison or jail, or on probation or parole.
- As of 1995, one in fourteen (7%) adult Black males was incarcerated in prison or jail on any given day, representing a dou-

bling of this rate from 1985. The 1995 figure for white males was 1%.

- A Black male born in 1991 has a 29% chance of spending time in prison at some point in his life. The figure for white males is 4%, and for Hispanics, 16%" (Mauer, 1999).

Mauer further points out that the Black proportion of violent arrests, although high, has virtually remained unchanged for 20 years.

A recent crime phenomenon that has come to the attention of many Americans in the last few years is that of "Driving While Black." This practice highlights the propensity of police to stop Black males while driving for alleged traffic violations. Often these practices were supported by the use of drug courier profiles. In central Florida researchers documented traffic stops made by police in the late 1990's and discovered that 70% of the drivers stopped were either African American or Hispanic. *This gives cause for concern especially when considering that African Americans only constitute 12% of the state's driving population.* "Black motorists stopped by the Houston Police Department are 3.5 times more likely to be searched than [whites], the worst disparity reported in any major Texas city, according to the first statewide compilation of statistics since law endowment agencies have been required to report racial data on traffic stops. Statewide, Blacks are 1.6 times more likely to be searched after being stopped then [whites]" (Rodriquez, 2004).

This practice is significant because it leads to the acquiring of a criminal record which, in the future, would significantly increase an individual's chances of becoming incarcerated (Mauer, 1999).

INCOME AS AN INDICATOR OF SOCIAL PROGRESS.

Gammon (2002) reports that according to 2000 U.S. Census data "whites earn nearly twice as much money as African Americans." In Oakland, he shares, the median household income among non-Latino whites was $57,399 compared to $31,185 for [B]lacks." Among Oakland families, he goes on, "the income divide was even more dramatic. The median white family income was $84,194 compared to $35,061 for [B]lack families." The case was not that much different in Berkeley as among "Berkeley white families…the annual median income was $95,571 a year while [B]lack families brought home only $37,855." When asked "Why are [B]lack people poorer?" Gammon reports that Debbie Reed, an economist with the Public Policy Institute of California who is studying income inequality responded with: "The real answer, the biggest answer, is that we don't know." Reed, again according to Gammon, reports that "other factors could come into play, such as the quality of schools children have access to, which could have more to do with class than race. Throughout the (school) system," Reed went on "the resources available to African-American children are very different from the resources available to non-Hispanic white children."

Skertic (2002) reports that extreme conditions coexist in an area of Chicago known as the Near South Side. In that area the income in half the African American households was less than $14,173 in 1999 and one in three people lived below the poverty line. Skertic contrasts these conditions with the fact that the median income in white households in the same area was $88,489 in 1999.

The working-poor individual or family consists of one or more who are employed, but still do not make a living wage as defined by the U.S. government's poverty line. For example, a full time minimum wage worker earns $2,000 less than the poverty threshold for a family of three. "African Americans are twice as likely to be working poor as white Americans: 15 percent of the Black community work far below poverty-level wages, versus 6 percent of whites. (However, in sheer numbers, there are more white working-poor Americans.) (Chideya, 1995).

Even though the income gap between whites and African Americans has narrowed in recent years, according to Genaro Armas, the change has been slight. On average a college educated white man earned about $65,000 in 2001 while a similarly educated white woman made 40% less, and African Americans and Hispanics earned 30% less according to Census Bureau estimates (Armas, 2003).

LONGEVITY AS AN INDICATOR OF SOCIAL PROGRESS.

Except at the very oldest ages, [B]lack Americans have the highest death rates of any of America's racial and ethnic groups (Ameristat, 2002b). Hoover cites a study of premature deaths carried out by the Cleveland (Ohio) Health Department. Operationally defining premature death as "the age [at which] someone dies subtracted from 65," the authors of the study found that "whites who died prematurely lost an average of 5.1 years, with cancer, heart disease and AIDS causing the most early deaths. Blacks lost 11.1 years, with infant mortality, homicide and cancer claiming the most lives prematurely." In Hoover's words, "Among those in the city who died before age 65 that year [1996,] [B]lacks lost twice as many years as whites (Hoover, 1999). Nation-wide, whites lived 5.6 years longer than [B]lacks in 2000" (Associated Press, 2002).

Further, the following is found in Chapter 2 of a 1999 United States Commission on Civil Rights report entitled *The Role Of Government And Private Health Care Programs And Initiatives, The Health Care Challenge: Acknowledging Disparity, Confronting Discrimination, And Ensuring Equality:*

o "Infant mortality rates are 2½ times higher for Blacks than for whites.

o Black men under age 65 have prostate cancer at nearly twice the rate of white men under age 65.

o The death rate for heart disease for [B]lacks is higher than for whites (147 deaths per 100,000, compared with 105 deaths per 100,000)."

Further from an editorial in the Wednesday, 20 November 2002 <u>Houston Chronicle</u>:

o African American women are nine times as likely as white women to die of AIDS, and

o [B]lack infants die at twice the rate of whites (p. 34.A).

WEALTH AS AN INDICATOR OF SOCIAL PROGRESS

Lee reports that "The Ohio State University [was asked to analyze] data from the Federal Reserve Board's 1998 Survey of Consumer Finances." The report found that while the "median household wealth among [B]lacks grew by 321 percent between 1989 and 1998, from $3,680 in 1989 to $15,500…that was still less than a quarter of the $71,000 accumulated by the typical American Household." The report found, according to Lee, that "24 percent of [B]lack Americans said they spend more than their income, compared with 14 percent of all Americans. Thirty-two percent of [B]lack Americans say they do not save, compared with 23 percent of All Americans" as well (Lee, 2000).

Snyder citing U. S. Census Bureau data reports that while the median income fell 2.2 percent in 2000, African Americans experienced about a 3 percent drop in income. Hispanics and whites experienced about a 1 percent drop in income in that same year (Snyder, 2002). The *Houston Defender*, citing a September, 2002 report released by the Commerce Department's Census Bureau sheds additional light on gaps in African American wealth versus white wealth. With respect to poverty, the *Defender* reports that for whites, "the poverty rate rose from 7.4 percent in 2000 to 7.8 percent in 2002." The poverty rate for African Americans remained at 22.7 percent. Regarding income, the *Defender* reports that for whites, "median household income declined 1.3 percent, in real terms between 2000 and 2001 to $46,305. For African Americans…the drop [was] 3.4 percent (a loss of $1,025) to $29,470 (Houston Defender, 2002).

Arthur Kennickell, a Senior Economist and Project Director on the Federal Reserve Board indicated that while African Americans constituted 13 % of the population they owned only 3% of the wealth. The typical white family had six times as much wealth as the typical Black family. Eighteen percent of white families and only 2% of Black families have a net worth of over half a million dollars. Of even greater concern was a comparison of the debt ratio between African American families and white families. Kennickell reported that the debt of the typical African American family was 30%, while the debt of the typical white family was on 11% of their assets (Kennickell, 2001).

INDIVIDUALS, ENVIRONMENTS, ORGANIZATIONS, AND CULTURAL PERFORMANCES

It is evident from this discussion of social progress indicators that the cultural performances of Americans of African Descent may not be judged as excellent. How then, do we explain the cultural performances of African Americans and their relationships to the attainment of cultural excellence in the context of outcomes of their interactions with American social systems? Let us construe cultures shared by Americans of African descent as a type of system by constructing them as an organization, locating that organization in the context of a social system, and investigating linkages between cultural performances and cultural excellence. Let us examine this model in terms of schools as an educational social system.

System theories emphasize the relationships that exist among individuals, groups, organizations or communities. There are several assumptions about social systems that make this model especially appropriate for this discussion. First, social systems are open. Schools are open as they are affected by the values of the community, politics and also history. Second, social systems involve people and people behave based on their needs and roles. This concept provides a way to interpret what occurs between individuals (Hoy & Miskel, 1996). It generally provides a broad perspective and describes and predicts dynamics that might occur.

A very popular and accepted view of organizations is the open-system perspective. This model views organizations as influenced by and dependent on the external environment. According to this perspective, organizations receive inputs (people, materials, and resources), transform them and produce outputs. (Hoy & Miskel, 1996). This model can be used to explain the relationship of American social systems to the external environment and the outcomes of interacting with these systems for Americans of African descent in relation to their interaction (either directly or indirectly) with this external environment.

Schools are open systems confronted with constraints that change as the environment changes, constantly adapting to different environmental elements. It is hoped and expected that children who enter the educational system will be transformed by the educational system into educated individuals who will contribute to society and enjoy a quality of life superior to that enjoyed by their parents (See Illustration I).

The most fundamental property of a system is the interdependence of its parts, variables, or subsystems. Systems can be made up of symbols, objects, and subjects that contribute to the pattern of behavior that exists within the system. Systems generally have the following characteristics:

o   They are highly organized
o   Boundaries are important.
o   Behaviors of individuals can't be understood without reference to the system to which they belong.
o   They are homeostatic.

o   They are goal directed. The goal is the self-preservation of the unit (Ruegger and Johns, 1996).

ILLUSTRATION I
A Perspective of The School As An Open System

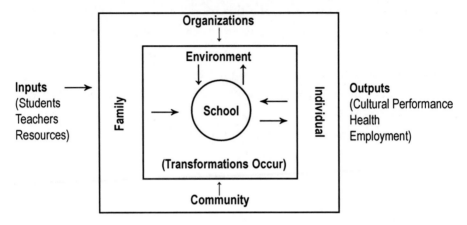

The systems approach provides a perspective for assessing various aspects of cultural performances. The interactions between people and the various systems, with which they have contact, have great impact upon human behavior. African Americans, as all human beings, are constantly involved with their social environments. Therefore it can be assumed that the cultural performances of African Americans are directly related to the various systems within which interactions occur (See Illustration II).

ILLUSTRATION II
Understanding The Dynamics of Human Behavior

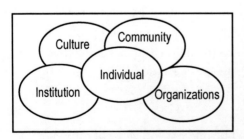

EXPLANATION OF TERMS

Culture – The sum total of artifacts which accumulate as a people struggle for survival and self determination.

Community- People who have something in common that connects them in some way and distinguishes them from others.

Institution – A custom or the behavioral patterns of a community such as marriage, justice, religion.

Organizations – Structural groups of people working towards a mutual goal and who perform established work activities.

Kettner, Daley and Nichols (1985) suggest two perspectives that also shed light on relationships among cultural performance phenomena, organizational theory and community theory. Organizational theory focuses on how organizations function and what motivates people to work towards organizational goals, and understanding the ability of an organization to accomplish its goals. Community theory refers to the nature of communities. Although communities provide people with necessary resources and support systems, they can also have a devastating effect on a resident's ability to function in a healthy way. In order to understand an individual's behavior, one must first understand how that individual feels and acts, individually as well as in relation to the particular subgroup (ethnic, gender, age) to which the individual belongs. One must also understand, as well, how other people, groups and organizations within the larger social environment, view the group to which the individual belongs. Within groups individuals have a tendency to lose their individual identity and assume the group identity. It is at this point that the characteristics of the group become the characteristics of the individual.

Pinderhughes in 1982 noted that slavery and oppression combined with racism and exclusion have produced a "victim system." Within a "victim system" self-esteem and problematic responses in communities and families are reinforced. Barriers limit the chance for achievement, which in turn leads to poverty or stress in relationships and limited opportunities for families to meet their own needs or improve their communities. This in turn contributes to social problems. The phenomenon described by Pinderhughes in 1982 still exists today in communities largely populated by African Americans.

Therefore, from the perspectives of the open system and organization and community theories, it is not difficult to see how relationships among the various groups and entities in the life of an individual can impact that individual's performance, his or her long-term success and or failure, and the cultural performances of the group to which the individual belongs. External factors and organizations, along with those things within a child's micro world particularly family, health, values and life experiences have a direct impact on a child's success or failure in school. It is widely concluded that school success will lead to positive life-decision choices and experiences such as employment, physical health, financial security and generally successful life experiences. It is also widely concluded that the failure of the school to educate will lead to unemployment, poor health, lack of financial security and a generally unsuccessful life. A successful or failing life cycle is begun or continued based on these experiences. The cultural performances of Americans of African descent and their ability to preserve self, reproduce self and care for its progeny is thus determined (See Illustration III).

ILLUSTRATION III
School Reform as it Relates to Cultural Excellence

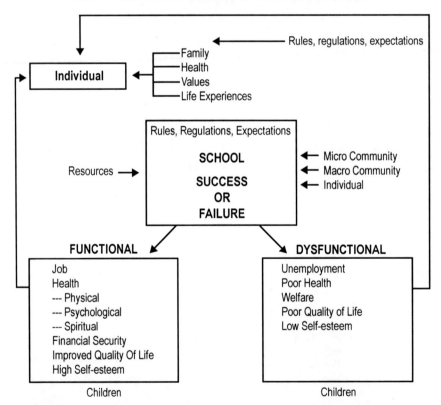

CONCLUSION

We began this chapter with a quotation from Ralph Ellison's *Juneteenth* and inserted a second quotation from the same novel just prior to discussing the four questions posed. We chose to quote liberally from Ellison because, in this novel, he so eloquently raises questions about extents to which the emancipation of Americans of African descent is real or an illusion. Concomitantly, Ellison lays open the way for self-emancipation by improving our cultural performances in such a way that where our culture performances are dysfunctional we strive toward functional excellence; and where our cultural performances are functional we strive toward cultural excellence. It is in that spirit and with that expectation that we conclude with this optimistic idea from *Juneteenth*:

> "Ah, my fair warrior, my cooing dove, we'll create possibility out of rags and bones and hanks of hair; out of silks and satins and bits of fur, out of gestures and inflections of voice and scents orchestrated funky-sweet; with emphatic nods and elusive sympathies and affirmations and every move to all of them a danced proclamation of 'I believe you can, I know you can; we can in faith achieve the purest dream of our most real realities –look upon us two and see your finest possibilities'"

(Ellison, 1999, pp. 72-73)

Note the emphasis on action: "I believe you can, I know you can; we can in faith achieve the purest dream of our most real realities…" William Greider, author of *Who Will Tell the People – The Betrayal of American Democracy*, picks up this theme with: "A democratic insurgency does not begin with ideas, as intellectuals presume, or even with great political leaders who seize the moment. It originates among the ordinary people who find the will to engage themselves with their surrounding reality and to question the conflict between what they are told and what they see and experience" (Greider, 1992). It is in that spirit and with respect for your points of view that we leave you to reflect on our fourth question: What steps or actions can be taken that will improve the cultural performances of Americans of African descent?

NOTES

(1) While it is acknowledged that the NABSE discussion of cultural excellence contains two elements: (1) how the group per-

forms culturally, and (2) extents to which the group is conscious of its history and culture, the authors made the decision to focus this chapter on the former element. The rationale for making this decision was that while little has been collected about the former, much is available about the latter.

(2) The research design, method, or strategy used in this chapter is known as descriptive research. This methodology was selected because it is congruent with the purpose of the study, which was to describe systematically, the facts and characteristics associated with the cultural performances of Americans of African descent, factually and accurately. To quote Issac and Michael, "Descriptive research is used in the literal sense of describing situations or events. It is the accumulation of a database that is solely descriptive – it does not necessarily seek or explain relationships, test hypotheses, make predictions, or get at meanings and implications, although research aimed at these more powerful purposes may incorporate descriptive methods. Research authorities, however, are not in agreement on what constitutes "descriptive research" and often broaden the term to include all forms of research except historical and experimental. In this broader context, the term survey study is often used to cover the examples listed above.

(3) It is pointed out that while Americans of African descent participate disproportionately in the various branches of the armed forces, their support for war is inversely disproportionate. Dyson observes that "As was the case with the Vietnam War, there was greater support of the Gulf War among whites than [B]lacks. A poll found that 83 percent of whites but only 43 percent of [B]lacks supported President Bush's decision to attack Iraq in the Persian gulf War." Dyson shares that "30 percent of American front-line soldiers in Saudi Arabia were [B]lack." As has already been seen, African Americans contributed 12.1 percent to the United States population at that point in time.

CHAPTER THREE

NECESSITY PLUS POSSIBILITY
School Performance with Children and Youth of African Descent and Resulting Performance Gap Identification

"All Boundaries down, freedom was not only the recognition of necessity, it was the recognition of possibility."

RALPH ELLISON

THE INVISIBLE MAN, P. 499

ABSTRACT

The purpose of this chapter is to examine two issues: "Is perceived improved school performance with children and youth of African descent an illusion?" and, "Why is perceived improved school performance not reflected in the preparation of African American learners for effective and satisfying participation in society?" The authors addressed these issues by analyzing school-performance data specific to the nation, to one state, and to one high school. It was found that commitment to a *Color-Blind* or to a *School-Improvement* paradigm, exclusively, may lead educational leaders to the erroneous conclusion that school performance with African American learners is improving. Discrepancies between how well schools prepare white versus African American children and youth to (a) competently perform such school tasks as reading and mathematics and (b) successfully transact the university and/or the world of work were found to be wide and persistent. An action taken, compatible with a *School-Improvement* exclusively paradigm and characterized by the political *necessity* to raise high-stakes test scores and a strategy compatible with a *School- Improvement* via *Gap-Identification* paradigm driven by *possibility* are summarized. The authors conclude with a call for additional initiatives consistent with the *School-Improvement* via *Gap-Identification* paradigm in order that the *necessity* for school improvement *and* improved life-chance *possibilities* for children and youth of African descent be realized.

INTRODUCTION

The National Alliance of Black School Educators (NABSE) is the nation's largest network of African American educators. NABSE is dedicated to improving results of schooling for children and youth of African descent. To that end, NABSE seeks, among other things, to promote and facilitate the education of all students (especially those of African descent) by ensuring high standards and quality in our public education systems. NABSE has articulated its perspective on these matters in the following terms: "We have a vision of quality education for the African American child... Contrary to some professional thinking, the capacity of African American children to learn is intact, in spite of the malignant neglect by...social, educational and other systems. The major problems are the problem of *resources* and the problem with the National, state and local *will* and *commitment* to insure that our children's needs are met"(NABSE, 1984, P. 11).

This vision of quality education is enlarged upon in a 1984 NABSE report entitled *Saving the African American Child* in the context of discussions of *Academic and Cultural Excellence*: "Quality education has to do with the *output* of ...educational institutions whose policies and practices contribute significantly to the intellectual, physical, and psychological preparation of individuals for effective and satisfying participation in society...In addition, quality education refers to the successful efforts of those educational institutions which provide major assistance to African American people in fulfilling needs to alter those elements of the social structure in ways that will promote equal opportunity for all in the society" (NABSE, 1984, Page 12).

The former attribute of quality education, *output*, conjures up Ellison's yoking of "freedom" *and* "the recognition of *necessity*." The subsequent attribute, the *school's role in promoting equal opportunity for all*, and Ellison's use of the liaison "not only" are reminiscent of his commingling of "freedom" and "the recognition of possibility." Both conditions, "necessity" *and* "possibility," are seen as precursors to freedom - a desired outcome of schooling. The subsequent attribute, the school's role in promoting equal opportunity for all and the recognition of *possibility*, may be invisible to educational leaders who are committed to *Color-Blind* and/or *School-Improvement* paradigms, exclusively, and who make educational policy decisions consistent with rules and regulations peculiar to those paradigms.

Taken together, the beliefs, values, and attitudes associated with "preparation of individuals for effective and satisfying participation in society" *and* "fulfilling needs to alter those elements of the social structure in ways that will promote equal opportunity for all in the society" (NABSE, 1984, p. 12) signal two key components of the *Cultural Excellence* construct: *survival and self-determination*. *Survival* includes the *"preservation of one's people and one's self, the reproduction of one's people and one's self, and the care of the progeny which result."* *Self-determination* refers to *"liberty, equality, and the pursuit of happiness."* *Cultural excellence* is effected when "the group's birth rate exceeds its death rate, infant mortality is below normal, the mortality rate of the group is superior to the average, and the progeny are more successful than the parent group in social progress using education, income, occupation, and the political office holders as indicators, and when the group is conscious of its history and culture" (NABSE, 1984, p.12-13). This quest for *Educational and Cultural Excellence* is encapsulated passionately by "We are determined to gain both academic and cultural *excellence*. Education for African Americans is now, as it always has been to us, a passport to the future. Our children will gain that prize with our help, with equality of opportunity in the nation, and with the help of Almighty God" (NABSE, 1984, p.12-13).

THE PROBLEM

The overarching purpose of this chapter is to better understand extents to which *Educational and Cultural Excellence* are being effected by the schools for children and youth of African descent. The authors approached this purpose by examining the belief commonly held by educational leaders that public school performance with children and youth of African descent is improving. This approach was deemed appropriate because of a real or apparent negative correlation between (a) perceived improved school performance (*Educational Excellence*) and (b) extents to which children and youth of African descent are prepared by the schools for effective and satisfying participation in society (*Cultural Excellence*). This discrepancy led the authors to examine four questions:

1. Is school performance with children and youth of African descent improving?
2. Are school performances with white and African American children and youth comparable?
3. Is school performance with children and youth of African descent comparable to school performances with children and youth of other ethnic groups, specifically children and youth of Hispanic, Asian, and Native American descent.
4. To what extent is perceived improved school performance with children and youth of African descent reflected in their preparation for effective and satisfying participation in society?

CONDITIONS AND PRACTICE

There appear to be two perspectives regarding the nature of the achievement gap and indicated gap reduction actions. One perspective blames the victim. The other calls on the nation's educational leaders to take responsibility for results of schooling associated with children and youth of African descent.

An example of the former may be found in North Carolina's House Bill 1547 entitled *Closing the Achievement Gap*. This act would address the gap by "assisting families at certain income levels with children performing below grade level in improving family cohesiveness, functioning, and economic progress and student academic success" (General Assembly of North Carolina). This "blame the victim" approach has been criticized by such practitioners as Kati Haycock, former Director of *The Education Trust*. In an article entitled *Can Current Education Reform Efforts close the growing Achievement Gap?*, she shares that "policies aimed at the family and the broader social environment have missed a critical element of why academic performance has diminished—low educational expectations for poor minority youth...

curricular tracking has a dramatic impact… A school's teachers and the standards to which its students are held also have a dramatic impact on student performance…as students in high-poverty schools are often taught by teachers who do not even have an undergraduate minor degree in the subject they teach (at a rate as high as 33 percent in some cities).…We have much lower standards for poor and minority students. This problem often starts even before formal education begins: 'In pre-school, [poor kids] do more coloring than reading and writing;'…. 'A' students in a high–poverty school achieve at about the same level as 'C' students in affluent schools" (Spera, 1997).

Haycock is quoted in a paper presented in December of 1998 at the California School Boards Association's annual meeting entitled *The Achievement Gap in California: Implications for a Statewide Accountability System* with the "basic reason why we have the gap …is not poverty. Rather, the reason is because we teach different children different things. Many …African American students get a lower-level, less rigorous curriculum; often assign the least qualified teachers to teach them; expect less of them, and that becomes a self-fulfilling prophecy." The paper goes on to report that "California ranks 50th in number of high school teachers with even a minor in the subject they teach, which is especially negative for math/science; urban, especially 'inner-city' schools have the hardest time attracting and keeping qualified teachers; and most of the emergency-permit teachers are in the urban districts" (McRobbie, 1998).

Lynn Olson (1996) authored an article that appeared in *Education Week on the WEB* in which it was reported that "Roughly 55 out of every 100 white and Asian-American students complete Algebra II and Geometry. Only 35 percent of African American …seniors take this math. Although one of every four white seniors takes physics, only one in six Black seniors…completes this course…. Blacks are much less likely than whites to go to college. For every 100 white Americans, nearly 60 attended college and 25 earned a bachelor's degree. Only 40 percent of Blacks attend college and just 12 percent earn a bachelor's degree by age 30" (Olson, 1996).

Olson states that "Five years ago…Providence, Rhode Island…began requiring…higher-level mathematics …Today, 97 percent of …African American students there take Algebra, compared with only 37 percent of African American students…in 1991"…"In Tennessee, 23 percent of public

K-12 students were African Americans in 1992, and 24 percent of students in Advanced Placement mathematics and science courses were African Americans. In Virginia, 26 percent of public K-12 students were African Americans, but only 7 percent of students in Advanced Placement mathematics and science courses were African Americans" (Olsen, 1996).

A second example was heralded by the superintendent of schools in Arlington Virginia: "urging more students to attend after-school and Saturday classes and summer school, as well as adding tutors and specialists in subjects such as reading" (Mathews, 1999). This approach, in effect, provides opportunities for students to get more of the same ineffective instruction received during normal class hours and provides teaching resources that might better be utilized in the normal instructional program: "This problem often starts even before formal education begins: 'In pre-school, [poor kids] do more coloring than reading and writing" (Haycock in Spera, 1997). This "problem" is highlighted in a 1998 National Center for Educational Statistics *Early Childhood Longitudinal Study* where gaps in the school's performances with African Americans and white students or, gapism, were found. Percentages of first time kindergarten students achieving proficiency in reading are shown in Table 1.

TABLE 1
Percentages of first time kindergarten students achieving proficiency in reading

Subjects	Proficiencies	Attainment Percentages	
		Blacks	whites
Reading	Letter Recognition	55	73
	Beginning Sounds	19	34
	Ending Sounds	10	20
Mathematics	Number and Shapes	90	96
	Relative Size	42	66
	Ordinal Sequence	09	26

Source: The Conditions of Education 2000 – Table f...d Proficiency in Reading and Mathematics http://nces.ed.gov/pubs2000/coe2000/ section2/s_table 11_1.html

Gaps identified in Table I may suggest "family and broader social environment" or "more time on task" policies to some. However, such a suggestion is found to contradict the NABSE position on the matter: "the capacity of African American children to learn is intact, in spite of the malignant neglect by...social, educational and other systems" (NABSE, 1984, p. 11). The Patterson Research Institute's *Data Book* provided assistance with regard to resolving this contradiction. On this issue they write "Three common criteria upon which children are assessed for school readiness include observations of their attitudes, their behavior, and their academic skills development" (Patterson, 1997, p. 10). The Institute goes on to report that a "higher percentage of African American (52.5) 3- and 4-year olds than of whites (43.5) [attended] some kind of preschool program" and present percentages of parents who participated in various preschool reinforcing activities at home (Table 2).

TABLE 2
Percentages of parents who participated in preschool reinforcing activities.

Activity	Black children	White children
In last week		
Told child a story	72.8	7.9
Taught Child Letters and Words	8.0	86.3
Taught Child songs and Music	72.2	72.8
Played with Toys and Games Indoors	94.4	90.7
In Last Month		
Visited Library	28.9	41.6
Went to Play, Concert. or Show	29.8	22.2
Took Child to Aquarium	17.0	15.4
Talked With Child about Ethnic Heritage	55.0	38.0

Source: Patterson, 1997, p. 21

With regard to "attitude," the Institute found that in most identified categories, learners of African descent had better school-specific attitudes than did white learners who were enrolled in Kindergarten (See Table 3). Regarding the behavior of these children, the Institute reports a mixed picture (See Table 4) but there does not appear to be meaningful differences in behavior between the two populations. With respect to academic skill development, the Institute presents data on reading levels of five-year-olds.

TABLE 3

Attitudes of African American versus white preschoolers.

Behavior	Black children	White children
Parent Said		
Complained About School	18.7	23.9
Reluctant to Go to School	13.2	18.7
Pretended to Be Sick	09.8	08.7
Says Good Things About School	95.6	95.8
Said Liked Teacher	93.1	96.4
Looked Forward to School	98.1	94.9
Teacher Said		
Child Gets Along Well With Others	91.4	89.5
Child is Enthusiastic	90.3	82.4
Child Lacks Confidence	16.5	13.5
Child Speaks Out in Class	63.6	60.3

Source: Patterson, 1997, p. 20-21

TABLE 4

Behavior of African Americana versus white preschoolers.

Abilities	Black children	White children
Identifies All Colors	62.9	83.7
Recognizes All Letters of the Alphabet	16.5	21.0
Counts up to 50 or higher	13.9	12.9
Writes First Name	42.2	47.5
Buttons Clothes	94.5	86.4
Holds Pencil Properly	94.2	89.5
Writes and Draws	66.6	64.5
Trips, Stumbles or Falls Easily	16.4	11.1
Is Afraid to Talk to Strangers	34.6	44.8
Has Short Attention Span	24.8	21.0
Began Speaking Late	14.89	16.1

Source: Patterson, 1997, p. 17

As shown in Table 5, African American 5-year-olds appeared to have been better developed than were white 5-year-olds in this respect. Given these data, the school's differential performances, discernible beginning in kindergarten, may not be laid at the steps of the parents of African descent. The capacity of African American children to learn is intact when they approach the schoolhouse door. Something is going on in the schoolhouse.

TABLE 5

Reading "levels" of African American versus white preschoolers.

Characteristics	Black children	White children
Can Read Books on Own	30.4	21.7
Does not read	69.6	78.3
Reads the Written Word	23.2	15.4
Pretends to Read	2.8	1.4
Does Both	4.3	4.9
Average Age in Months Started to Read	60	64

Source: Patterson, 1997, p. 23

METHOD

Examining data and developing outcomes-of-schooling cases specific to the national, state and local levels resulted in responses to the study questions. National Assessment of Educational Progress (NAEP) data 1971-1998 (selected years) were consulted. Texas Assessment of Academic Skills (TAAS) data were used as bases for responses to the study questions at the state level. "Results of the ACT 2000 Assessment," a memorandum from the superintendent of schools addressed to members of the local school board, a school-specific high school profile data sheet, two matrices entitled "Test Score Comparison," the high school Curriculum Bulletin (2000-2001,) data sheets provided by the school's principal, and course specific class lists were consulted in the process of developing responses to the study questions at the local (high school) level. These questions were examined within the boundaries of *Color-Blind, School-Improvement*, exclusively, and a *Gap-Identification* paradigm.

TABLE 6

Average school performance for 1990, 1992, 1994, and 1998: Reading and Mathematics, by grade for all students.

Subjects	Grades	School Years			
		1990	1992	1994	1998
Reading	4		217	214	217
	8		260	260	264
	12		292	287	291
Mathematics	4	213	220	224	
	8	263	268	272	
	12	294	300	304	

Source: The Conditions of Education 2000 – Section...Performance of Students in Grades 4, 8, and 12; wysiwyg://56/http://nces.ed.gov/pubs2000/ coe2000/ section2/ indicator 13. gtml

RESULTS AT THE NATIONAL LEVEL

It may be seen from Table 6 that the *Color-Blind* response was mixed to the question: Is school performance with children and youth of African descent improving? While no meaningful differences in reading performances between 1992 and 1998 were evident, small positive differences in mathematics performances were found. A somewhat different picture emerged when NAEP data were examined from a *School-Improvement* paradigm, exclusively, the reading response was positive (See Table 7). School performance improved by 80 points with African Americans in grade 4, by 78 points with African Americans in grade 8, and 76 points with African Americans in grade 12 students. However, the rate of improvement was not in the desired direction. The *School-Improvement* paradigm, exclusively, the Mathematics response was that school performance improved by 79 points with African American grade 4, 83 points with African American grade 8 and 80 points with African American grade students (See Table 7, page 60). This appears to be a relatively positive response to this question until the African American–white comparability question was answered. Again, it is seen from Table 7 that, with respect to reading, the results-of-schooling gap between African American and white children and youth was reduced from a little more than 30 to a little less than 30 scale points during the data period. However, African American 8th graders continuously scored below white 4th graders and African American 12th graders

58

TABLE 7
Average school performance for 1990, 1992, 1994, and 1998: Reading, and Mathematics, by grade for all, African American, and white students.

Subjects	School Years											
	1990			1992			1994			1998		
Grades	4	8	12	4	8	12	4	8	12	4	8	12
Reading												
All Students				217	214	217	260	260	264	292	287	291
AA students				193	187	194	238	237	243	273	265	270
Difference				24	27	23	22	23	21	19	22	21
White students				225	224	227	267	268	272	298	294	298
Difference				32	37	33	29	31	29	25	29	28
Mathematics												
All Students	213	220	224	263	268	272	294	300	304			
AA students	189	193	200	238	238	243	268	276	280			
Difference	24	27	24	25	30	29	26	24	24			
White students	225	224	227	267	268	272	298	294	295			
Difference	36	31	27	29	30	29	30	18	15			

Source: The Conditions of Education 2000 – Section...Performance of Students in Grades 4,8, and 12; wysiwyg://56/http://nces.ed.gov/pubs2000/coe2000/section2/indicator13.gtml

continuously scored below white 8th graders. Regarding mathematics, the school performance gap between African American and white students remained at or around 30 points at grade 4. African American students in the 12th grade consistently scored below white 8th graders. Thus the response to the question: "Are school performances with white and African American children and youth comparable?" was in the negative.

Table 8 (page 61) reveals that with respect to reading, school performance was least effective with children and youth of African descent. The school's performance with African American 12th graders resulted in scores lower than the scores of Asian/Pacific Islanders, Native Americans, and Hispanics (with the exception of 992, Hispanics only). Further, African American 12th graders continuously scored below Asian/Pacific Islanders and Native Americans 8th graders. Regarding mathematics, the school's performance resulted in African American students scoring lower than Hispanic, Asian, and Native American students at each of the three grade levels during each school for which data were available. The school's performance with Asian/Pacific Islanders, Native Americans, and Hispanic children versus with children and youth of African descent were not comparable.

Admission of African American students to and completion of college

TABLE 8

Average school performance for 1990, 1992, 1994, and 1998: Reading, and Mathematics, by grade for all and specific categories of students.

Subjects / School Years

Grades	1990			1992			1994			1996			1998		
	4	8	12	4	8	12	4	8	12	4	8	12	4	8	12
Reading															
All Students				217	214	217	260	260	264				292	287	291
White students				225	224	227	267	268	272				298	294	298
Asian/Pac./Isl.				214	229	225	270	268	271				292	280	289
Nat. Am./				207	201	202	251	251	248				*	275	276
Hispanic				201	191	196	241	240	244				278	270	275
AA students				193	187	194	238	237	243				273	265	270
Mathematics															
All Students	213	263	294				220	268	300	224	272	304			
White students	220	270	301				228	278	306	232	282	311			
Asian/Pac./Isl.	228	279	311				232	289	316	232	274	319			
Nat. Am./	208	246	*				211	255	*	216	264	297			
Hispanic	198	244	276				202	247	284	206	251	287			
AA students	189	238	268				193	238	276	200	243	280			

Source: The Conditions of Education 2000 – Section…Performance of Students in Grades 4,8, and 12; wysiwyg://56/http://nces.ed.gov/pubs2000/coe2000/section2/indicator13.gtml

are critical instruments by which *Cultural Excellence* may be effected. While Table 9 does not provide sufficient data to answer the question, using the *Color-Blind* paradigm, it is clear that, from the perspective of the *School-Improvement* paradigm, exclusively, that there has been some improvement in school performance with respect to African American students taking the core and Advanced Placement (AP) examinations.

TABLE 9

Comparisons of school performances with African American versus white students: advanced course participation, advanced placement examination participation, enrollment in college and completion of the bachelor's degree.

	1971	1972	1982	1984	1994	1996	1997
Proportions of students who took core.							
White students			16		54		
AA students			12		45		
Difference			04		09		
Numbers of (12th grade) students (per 1000) who took AP examinations.							
White students				48		133	
AA students				08		32	
Difference				40		101	
Percentages of high school graduates (ages 16-24) who enrolled in college the October following graduation.							
White students			50		67		
AA students			46		56		
Difference			04		11		
Percentages of high school graduates (ages 25-29) who enrolled in college.							
White students	45						68
AA students	31						54
Difference	14						14
Percentages of high school graduates who finished four or more years of college.							
White students	23						35
AA students	12						16
Difference	11						19

Source: Sable, Jennifer. (1998). "The Educational Progress of Students."
http://nces.ed.gov/pubs98/condition98/c98003.html.

There are, however, at least two major problems with this conclusion. First, *The Conditions of Education* (1998,) referring to *A Nation at Risk* (1983), lists the courses that comprise the core curriculum (referred to as "the New Basics"): "4 years of English, and 3 years each of social studies, science, and mathematics." *The Conditions of Education* (1998) goes on to indicate that "Students who take rigorous academic course loads during high school have higher educational achievement than those who take a less rigorous curriculum independent of their social background. Students with higher levels of academic achievement are also more likely to attend college within 2 years following graduation independent of their social background" (Sable, 1998, Page 8). It may be seen from Table 10 that the *Nation at Risk* core is left wanting when compared to standards the schools are expected to meet for "virtually all African American children" by NABSE.

TABLE 10

Criterion levels of performance in basic subjects expected to be reached by the schools for African American students by the end of twelfth grade.

Subjects	Criterion Performances
Mathematics	Algebra in the sixth grade and calculus by the twelfth grade.
Economics	An understanding of and the ability to discuss the workings of the American and other economic systems.
Political Science	An understanding of and the ability to discuss the workings of the American political system.
Computer Competence	Ability to write computer programs in one or more languages
History	An understanding of and the ability to discuss African American perspectives on standard historical topics commonly taught in schools.
Language Arts	To be able to write a term research paper demonstrating the ability to use common English, appropriate documentation of idea, and appropriate presentation of ideas.
Foreign Language	A speaking, reading and writing knowledge of at least one foreign language. The acquisition of competence in an African language should be available as an option.
Science	A passing grade in a course equivalent to general chemistry. This assumes that the common practice is to require appropriate coursework in biology and physical sciences as prerequisites.
Vocational	Typing, childcare, work habits, employability.
African American History and Culture	Ability to tell the general story of Africans and African American people from earliest times to the present.

Source: National Alliance of School Educators. (1984). Saving the African American Child. Washington, D.C. Pages 35-36.

A second major problem with this core and Advanced Placement conclusion is that the gap between the school's performance with African American versus white students taking the core and Advanced Placement examinations, increased by 5 and 61 points, respectively (See Table 9). Again, Table 9 does not provide sufficient data to answer questions regarding percentages of high school graduates (ages 16-24) who enrolled in college the October following graduation, percentages of high school graduates (ages 25-29) who enrolled in college, or percentages of high school graduates who finished four or more years of college, using the *color-blind* paradigm. However, it is clear, from the perspective of the *School-Improvement* paradigm, exclusively, that there has been some improvement in school performance with African American students in terms of these three phenomena. It would be a mistake, however, to formulate educational policy consistent with these outcomes as the gap between the school's performance with African American versus white students with regard to these matters has either increased or remained stable (See Table 9).

RESULTS AT THE STATE LEVEL

If "a rising tide lifts all boats," and if over a seven-year period, the percentage of all students passing all Texas Assessment of Academic Skills (TAAS) tests taken increased by 24 points, it was likely that school performance with African American learners was improving. From the perspective of the *School-Improvement* paradigm, exclusively, it was found from Table 11 that percentages of African American students passing the reading and mathematics TAAS tests increased by approximately 21 and 39 points, respectively. It was also noted that meaningful reductions in differences between outcomes of schooling for African American versus white students produced by Texas schools were effected.

The veracity of the response to question #1: Is school performance with learners of African descent improving? was challenged, however, by the reality that in the three cases, (all TAAS tests taken, the TAAS reading test and the TAAS mathematics test) results for African American learners in the year 2000 were inferior to those generated by the school for white children seven years earlier (in the case of mathematics, six years). Observed improvement over the seven year data period may be a creature of how *poorly* Texas schools performed with African American learners prior to and including 1994 (Table 11).

TABLE 11

Percentages of all students passing reading, mathematics and all Texas Assessment of Academic Skills (TAAS) tests taken, 1994-2000.

Students	Subjects		1994	1995	1996	1997	1998	1999	2000*	Change 1994-2000
						School Years				Change
All Students	All Tests		55.6	60.7	67.1	73.2	77.7	78.3	79.9	+24.3
White	All Tests		69.4	74.8	79.8	84.9	87.9	87.9	89.3	+19.9
African Amer.	All Tests		33.3	38.3	46.9	55.7	62.6	64.0	68.0	+34.7
Difference			36.1	36.5	32.9	29.2	25.3	23.9	21.3	
All Students	Reading		76.5	78.4	80.4	84.0	87.0	86.5	87.4	+10.9
White	Reading		87.2	88.4	90.0	92.4	94.2	93.7	94.3	+7.1
African Amer.	Reading		60.2	63.0	66.8	73.2	78.2	78.2	80.8	+20.6
Difference			27.0	25.4	23.2	19.2	16.0	15.5	13.5	
All Students	Mathematics		60.5	65.9	74.2	80.1	84.2	85.7	87.4	+26.9
White	Mathematics		73.3	79.2	85.0	89.5	91.9	92.5	93.6	+20.3
African Amer.	Mathematics		38.1	43.8	55.0	64.1	70.5	72.8	77.0	+38.9
Difference			35.2	35.4	30.0	25.4	21.4	19.7	16.6	

*Beginning in 2000, results include Spanish grades 5 and 6, and grade 4, writing test takers.

Source: Texas Education Agency. Selected State Academic Excellence Indicator System Data. Seven Year History, 1994-2000.

RESULTS AT THE LOCAL LEVEL

Outcomes of a review of data from a high school in Florida contributed to our database at the local level. Staff and student characteristics are first discussed for background and context. Student membership (1999-2000) is provided in Table 12 where it is seen that African American students accounted for 40 percent of the student membership.

TABLE 12

Contributions of categories of students, by grade, to student membership

Grade	African American		White		Hispanic		Asian/Indian Multiracial		Total
	Numb.	%	Numb.	%	Numb.	%	Numb.	%	Numb.
09	561	42	194	15	546	41	31	2	1332
10	527	40	235	18	524	40	26	2	1312
11	287	38	123	16	327	43	27	4	763
12	230	39	110	19	230	39	13	2	583
Total	1605	40	662	17	1627	41	97	2	3991

Source: School fact sheet provided by principal, September 2000.

It may be seen from Table 13 that the contribution of African American students to the student membership was not reflected in the ethnic distribution of the staff. While the principal is of African descent, she (a) surrounded herself, disproportionately, with non-African American administrative and classroom leadership and, (b) again disproportionately, with African American non-educators. Table 13 shows that 75 percent of the school's assistant principals, 87 percent of the classroom teachers, 76 percent of "exceptional" student teachers, 78 percent of counselors, 100 percent of librarians, and 73 percent of teacher aides are not of African descent.

TABLE 13
Staff Characteristics

	African American		White		Hispanic		Asian/Indian Multiracial		Total
	Numb.	%	Numb.	%	Numb.	%	Numb.	%	Numb.
Principal	1	100	0	0	0	0	0	0	1
Assistant Principal	1	25	2	50	1	25	0	0	4
Classroom Teachers	19	13	93	64	32	22	1	1	145
Excep. Student Tchers	8	24	18	55	7	21	0	0	33
Guidance Counselor	2	22	5	56	2	22	0	0	9
Librarians	0	0	2	100	0	0	0	0	2
Teacher aides	3	27	6	55	2	18	0	0	11
Clerical/Secretaries	6	50	5	42	1	8	0	0	12
Custod/Service Wrkrs	15	68	1	5	6	27	0	0	22
Other	0	0	3	75	0	0	1	25	4

Source: School fact sheet provided by principal, September 2000.

It may also be found at Table 13 that 50 percent of clerks and secretaries and 68 percent of custodians/service workers are of African descent. This bi-modal distribution raises questions in view of the fact that African American students contribute 40 percent of the student membership. It will later be seen from Table 18 that this apparent structural bias against persons of African descent in this high school is pervasive.

Given available school-specific data and information, the question: Is school performance with children and youth of African descent improving? was responded to with difficulty. Ninety and ninety-one percent of grade 10 students scored at level 3 (passing) or above on the Florida Writing Assessment (Expository and Persuasive combined) in 1998 and 1999, respectively. Only 24 and 45 percent of 1999 grade ten students scored at level 3 or above on the 1999 Florida Comprehensive Assessment (reading and mathematics) Tests, respectively (School fact sheet provided by principal, September 2000). Again, using the "rising tide lifts all boats" metaphor, the *Color-Blind* response to this question was mixed. From the perspective of the *School-Improvement* paradigm, exclusively, the response to this question was in the negative. It is seen from Table 14 that school performance with African American students diminished in both reading and mathematics during the period 1999-2000 as measured by the Florida Comprehensive Assessment Tests.

TABLE 14

Performances of all, African American and white students on the Florida Comprehensive Assessment Reading and Mathematics Tests, 1999 and 2000.

Students	Subjects	School Years		Change
		1999	2000	1999-2000
State	Reading	306	298	-08
District	Reading	292	282	-10
School (All Students)	Reading	302	293	-09
White	Reading	320	310	-10
African American	Reading	288	285	-03
Difference		32	25	
State	Mathematics	308	306	-02
District	Mathematics	296	291	-05
School (All Students)	Mathematics	312	311	+01
White	Mathematics	324	331	+07
African American	Mathematics	296	293	-03
Difference		28	38	

Source: Test Score Comparison fact sheet provided by principal, September 2000.

Differences in outcomes of schooling for African American versus white and all students were clearly evident. It may be seen from Table 14 that the gaps between the school's performance with African American versus white students with respect to reading and mathematics were substantial. Meaningful gaps between the school's performance with African American versus white students with respect to reading and mathematics were found when Stanford Achievement Test results were examined as well. It may be seen from Table 15 that reading and mathematics outcomes of schooling gaps in school performances with African American versus white students were wide and enduring. Substantial gaps identified when school's performances with African American and white students in core subject areas measured by academic area grade averages are observed in Table 16 as well. The gaps in each academic area as well as grade point averages were substantial.

TABLE 15

Performances of all and categories of students on the Stanford Achievement Test Eighth Edition, 1997 Spring Administration, Reading Comprehension and Mathematics.

Reference groups	Reading		Mathematics	
	Grades	Median Percentiles	Grades	Median Percentiles
School	09	31	09	34
	11	37	11	40
	All Grades	34	All Grades	36
African American	09	23	09	23
	11	24	11	33
	All Grades	23	All Grades	27
White	09	56	09	54
	11	55	11	59
	All Grades	55	All Grades	56
Hispanic	09	34	09	34
	11	35	11	40
	All Grades	35	All Grades	36

Source: Data and Information sheet provided by principal, September 2000.

As already seen at Table 15, the school's performances with Hispanic students was superior to its performances with students of African descent with respect to reading and mathematics as measured by scores on the Stanford Achievement Test. End of course and Grade Point Averages for Students of African descent and for students in a category called "Other Minority" are presented in Table 16 (page 70). The gap in school performance was evident with respect to each core subject and grade point averages as well.

TABLE 16

Comparisons of school produced high school academic area grade averages of students of African descent and white students.

Reference Groups	Academic Areas		High School GPAs		
	English	Mathematics	Social Studies	Natural Science	
Total	2.71	2.67	2.73	2.75	2.71
African American	2.45	2.44	2.56	2.43	2.45
White	2.88	2.76	2.80	2.98	2.85
Differences	0.45	0.32	0.24	0.55	0.40
"Other" Minorities"	2.88	2.82	2.88	2.93	2.88
Differences	0.45	0.38	0.32	0.50	0.43

Source: Data and Information sheet provided by principal, September 2000.

The gap between African American and "Other Minority" students was greater than was the gap between African American and white students in mathematics and social studies and with respect to grade point averages. These findings led the authors to conclude that school performance with children and youth of African descent was not comparable to school performance with children and youth of other ethnic groups, specifically children and youth of Hispanic, Asian, and Native American descent."

As shown in Table 17, combined *less than core* and *more than core* scores for Asian American, Mexican American, Puerto Rican, and white students were *higher* than *more than core* means of African American students. These findings taken together with the fact that *more than core* and *less than core* means for African American students were not meaningfully different raised questions as to the value added by taking the core for African American students in this school.

The extent to which school performance with learners of African descent is reflected in preparation for effective and satisfying participation in society may also be discerned by inspecting Table 18. While keeping in mind that African Americans contributed 40 percent of the student membership (Table 12, page 66), it is seen from Table 18 (page 72), that African American students accounted for 16 percent of the CISCO Networking Academy enrollment, "a cooperative venture between educational institutions and CISCO, the world leader in networking for the Internet" (Cur-

TABLE 17

Average ACT scores for various reference groups: 2000 Assessment.

Reference Groups	English	Mathematics	Reading	Science	Composite Reasoning
Nation — All Tested Students	20.5	20.7	21.4	21.0	21.0
Florida — All Tested Students	19.9	20.5	21.0	20.4	20.6
The School District — All Tested Students	17.9	19.1	19.0	18.7	18.8
The School — All Tested Students	18.2	19.4	19.4	19.0	19.2
African American					
Core or more	17.5	19.0	18.1	18.0	18.2
Less than core	14.8	16.1	15.6	16.1	15.7
Total	16.7	18.2	17.3	17.3	17.5
Asian American					
Core or more	22.3	24.0	25.5	23.5	24.0
Less than core	*	*	*	*	*
Total	22.3	24.0	25.5	23.5	24.0
Mexican American					
Core or more	20.0	22.0	22.3	18.7	21.0
Less than core	*	*	*	*	*
Total	20.0	22.0	22.3	18.7	21.0
Puerto Rican					
Core or more	19.0	21.0	20.7	20.5	20.4
Less than core	14.0	16.4	17.3	17.3	16.4
Total	17.9	20.0	19.9	19.8	19.6
White					
Core or more	21.7	20.9	22.8	21.8	21.9
Less than core	19.0	17.5	19.0	17.5	18.5
Total	21.5	20.6	22.7	21.5	21.7

* Not Available.

Source: Data and information sheet provided by principal, September 2000. Memorandum to members of the district's school board from the superintendent of schools dated 17 August 2000 the subject of which was "Results of the ACT 2000 Assessment.

riculum Bulletin, 2000-2001, p. 22). CISCO, the world leader in networking for the Internet, has "cooperative ventures with educational institutions."

TABLE 18

Distribution of African American students among school academies.

Academies	Total Enrollment	African American Enrollment	% African American Enrollment
CISCO	58	9	15.5
Humanities	568	119	20.95
Child Care	129	68	52..7
Food Arts	128	68	53.1

Sources: Curriculum Bulletin, 2000-2001, Data and information sheet provided by principal, September, 2000

The question must be raised as to why African American students accounted for 40 percent of the student population but only 16 percent of the enrollment in this Academy. This is a particularly germane question in view of the widely acknowledged digital divide.

African American students accounted for 21 percent of the students enrolled in the Humanities Academy (See Table 18), "a strong interdisciplinary program involving the Language Arts and Social Studies Departments" (Curriculum Bulletin, 2000-2001, p. 21). The question must be raised as to why African American students accounted for only 21 percent of the Humanities Academy enrollment?

African American students accounted for 53 percent of the students enrolled in the Academy of Early Childhood Education and for 53 percent of the students enrolled in the Food Arts Academy (located, structurally, under "Family and Consumer Science"). The question must be raised as to why African American students accounted for 40 percent of the student population but 53 percent of the enrollment in these two courses of study designed to prepare students for minimum-wage jobs. Clearly, the evidence required that our response to this question be in the negative.

SUMMARY OF RESULTS

Question #1 was: "Is school performance with children and youth of African descent improving?" The *Color-Blind* response to the question at the

National level was mixed. Between 1992 and 1998, no meaningful differences in reading performances were evident and small positive differences in mathematics performances were found. It was likely, given the data at the state level, that school performance with African American learners was improving. From the *School- Improvement*, exclusively, perspective at the national level there would appear to have been improvement in reading. However, the magnitude of improvement in reading was not in the desired direction.

There was no discernible improvement in school mathematics performance. At the state level, from the perspective of the *School-Improvement* paradigm, exclusively, it was found that percentages of African American students passing the reading and mathematics TAAS tests increased by approximately 21 and 39 points, respectively. Therefore meaningful reductions in differences between outcomes of schooling for African American versus white students produced by Texas schools had been effected. At the local level, the *Color-Blind* response to this question was mixed. From the perspective of the *School-Improvement* paradigm, exclusively, the response to this question was in the negative.

Question #2 was "Are school performances with white and African American children and youth comparable?" The response to this question at the National level was in the negative. At the state level, outcomes for African American learners in the year 2000 were inferior to those generated by the schools for white children seven (in the case of mathematics, six) years earlier. Differences in outcomes of schooling for African American versus white and all students were clearly evident at the local level.

Question #3 was " Is school performance with children and youth of African descent comparable to school performances with children and youth of other ethnic groups, specifically children and youth of Hispanic, Asian, and Native American descent?" The school's performances with Asian/ Pacific Islanders, Native Americans, and Hispanic children versus with children and youth of African descent at the national and state levels were found to be incomparable. School performance with children and youth of African descent was incomparable to school performance with children and youth of other ethnic groups, specifically children and youth of Hispanic, Asian, and Native American descent at the local level.

Question # 4 was "To what extent is perceived improved school performance with children and youth of African descent reflected in their preparation for effective and satisfying participation in society?" At the national level, the gap between the school's performance with African American students versus white students with regard to these matters has either increased or remained stable. Vast gaps in school processes and products designed to effect the preparation of African American versus white students for higher education or the world of work were found at the state level. At the local level, African American participation in high and low prestige courses of study were incommensurate with the extent to which they contributed to the student membership.

DISCUSSION

Color blindness results from a mindscape that avoids in practice and policy the societal distinction associated with race, class, gender, and age. While the impact of this condition is uneven, it results in claims of progress or growth that are in sharp contrast to realities. While the traditional examination of school achievement data reveals differences between subgroups of students in dissagregated databases, conventional wisdom accompanied by renewed interest and increased investments embrace school improvement philosophies over zero gap reduction possibilities.

How can a nation be prosperous in economics and moral in education at the same time? Speaking from the perspective of African Americans and possible psychological implications for the *Color-Blind* paradigm, Farber quotes the late James Farmer: "America would only become color blind when we gave up our color. The white man, who presumably has no color, would have to give up only his prejudices. We would have to give up our identities" (Farber 1967, p. 22).

How does one determine the impact of "color blindness" in a school or district that purports to honor and celebrate diversity? Due principally to the nature of organizational life and the social milieu that surrounds institutions of schooling throughout the country, it is necessary to divide before adding. This simple mathematical metaphor serves to illustrate how viewing student achievement data from two perspectives can have a profound influence on the data and the interpretations derived. For example, when examining student academic achievement data across diverse populations, it is necessary to disaggregate data in order to determine the effects of schools and programs on the groups comprising the diverse populations. This view enables the observer to detect patterns, trends, strengths, and weaknesses in the schools or programs that may be specific to a subgroup in the population. Short of this analysis, one is liable to assume generalizations that are not attributable to all groups in such a diverse population. If decision making is data-driven, the assumptions upon which the interpretations are based will be wrong or faulty at best. This leads to the conclusion that one must see color (divide) before critical analysis and problem solving can proceed.

Effective school people are seen as those who can analyze through division and problem solve through addition. What they derive from the analysis are facts about the subgroups that facilitate planning for the whole group (addition). If they are able to see color initially, color blindness in the implementation and maintenance of effective practices and programs may be productive and attainable.

The differences can be illustrated by examining the distance between *school- improvement* paradigms, exclusively, and *gap-reduction* concepts that are often applied to standards-based school reform. As mentioned above, even if the goal is to reduce the student achievement gaps between African American and white students, improved student academic achievement across the groups could conceivably result in gap expansion.

The concept of seeing color through the disaggregation of student assessment data has some applications that produce interesting accountability revelations. For example, one state that is nationally recognized for demonstrating improvement in student test scores under closer examination has actually widened the academic performance gap between African American and white students. Apparently, the analysis of success focused on test score improvement without adequate attention being given to reducing the gap to zero between African American student and white student academic performance. This oversight can produce the euphoric conclusion that school reform efforts are succeeding in addressing excellence and equity in student performance. While the zero gap reduction, which adds guarantees to equity, policies get short shrift in the rush to judgment about progress. Public policy can turn on performance or politics in this scenario and create bluster that ends up mirroring the assertion of "much ado about nothing."

The glaring examples occur in all areas of student testing in one state when 1997-2000 student achievement data are reviewed. In 2000, the gaps between African American and white students are clearly persistent. For example, in reading the gap is 13.5%, in mathematics the gap is 16%, and in writing the gap is 11.6%. When 1997 data are reviewed, the presence of these persistent gaps are confirmed. For example, the gap in reading was 19.2%, in mathematics the gap was 25.4%, and in writing the gap was 16.4%. Although there has been improvement in percentages of students passing state assessment measures and modest reduction over the four-year span, the double-digit gap between African American and white students continues to be a challenge for excellence and equity in the state's accountability system. This condition along with analyzed data validates the necessity to consider school reform policies that are driven by disaggregated data and issues related to a zero gap reduction paradigm, rather than a *School-Improvement* paradigm, exclusively (See Table 19).

TABLE 19

Percentage of students statewide meeting or exceeding the standard.

Subject	Reference Groups	1997	1998	1999	2000
Mathematics	All Students	80.1%	84.2%	85.7%	87.4%
	African American	64.1%	70.5%	72.8%	77.0%
	White	89.5%	91.9%	92.5%	93.6%
Writing	All Students	85.3%	87.4%	88.2%	88.2%
	African American	76.1%	80.4%	81.9%	82.4%
	White	92.5%	93.4%	93.1%	94.0%

Source: Texas Education Agency. 1999-2000 State Performance Report. State Academic

These data are used to fortify the case against *Color-Blind* approaches to policy and decision making until a level playing and performance field has been established between and within student cohort groups in schools and districts. Borrowing from a medical metaphor which posits that an untreated illness does not just disappear, this dilemma suggests that while the improvement paradigm is a major step in the right direction, it is representative of only the "first steps in a thousand miles journey" toward the zero gap reduction paradigm. Difficult though it may be, the positioning of educational reform on the state and national agendas offers great hope for appropriate school renewal efforts that produce quality, equity, and legitimacy for the students whom professionals are privileged to serve in the public education enterprise.

Necessary insights created by viewing disaggregated data sets (seeing color) seem to enhance the ability to create an appropriate response to the challenges of excellence for the aggregate data set (color blindness). Nel described the Cummins' model for teacher education as being particularly sensitive to the issue of student assessment (Nel, 1992, p. 38-39). Cummins (1986) asserted that basic change is needed in the underlying structure of traditional psychological assessment processes. He stated further that teacher effectiveness must deliver knowledge about the importance of, and how to become advocates of, minority students in assessment procedures (Cummins, 1986, p. 18-36). This guidance is critical as more and more states have embraced high stakes accountability systems in response to the standards based school reform movement.

PRIOR EFFORTS

Consistent with the authors embracing of a *School-Improvement* paradigm, exclusively, at earlier points in their careers, they previously designed and oversaw the implementation of a state-wide program designed to improve scores on a state-mandated criterion referenced test of African American children and youth from low income families in Texas. Essential elements of the program included capacity building, hosting forums for sharing best practices, providing on-sight technical assistance, exposing parents, administrators, community and religious leaders, and teachers to the thinking of nationally recognized practitioner-scholars of African descent, recognizing exemplary students, faculties and administrators, and disseminating newsletters and books of readings.

After three years of implementation, results for African American students from low-income families enrolled in participating middle schools exceeded expectations. While there was some improvement in the scores of African American students from low-income families enrolled in participating elementary schools, the gap between how well African American versus white students were prepared to perform on the state-mandated test maintained, and in some cases widened.

A PARADIGM SHIFT AND A NEW DIRECTION

The equal protection clause and other clauses should serve to guarantee equity in treatment of all citizens. Because equity in treatment has not yet come, it has been consistently necessary for African Americans to appeal to the courts and legislatures for protection in all areas of social life including education (NABSE, 1984, Page 16). After much discernment and review of the literature and of products of analyses of data reported above, the authors experienced a paradigm shift from *a School-Improvement* paradigm, exclusively, to a *School- Improvement* via *Gap-Reduction-to-Zero* paradigm. Embracing this paradigm has made it possible for the authors to envision and address the need to identify gaps in achievement, examine probable causes of identified gaps, engage in causal analysis, and invent strategies that, if implemented, would result in *School-improvement* via *Gap-Reduction-to-Zero* in Texas. The authors find it interesting that had they not experience their paradigm shifts; they would have remained committed to a unitary *School-Improvement* paradigm, exclusively. Having experienced this paradigm shift, the authors find themselves free to change their game plan and pursue *School-Improvement via Gap-Reduction-to-Zero* paradigm-based strategies.

One such strategy involves working with the Texas Alliance of Black School Educators (TABSE), the Texas affiliate of NABSE. TABSE is dedicated to effecting equal results of schooling for children and youth of African descent in Texas. A position paper entitled *Education of Children and Youth of African Descent in the State of Texas* was written, approved and disseminated to the TABSE membership. The position paper is being used to advocate for the accommodation of the natures and needs of learners of African descent by varying school conditions and practices and serving as the Affiliate's platform for *School-Improvement via Gap-Reduction-to-Zero* in the state of Texas by way of way of legislative remedy.

In the course of developing this Chapter, the authors examined several reports that shed light on our decision to embrace a *School-Improvement via Gap-Reduction-to-Zero* paradigm. In several ways, these reports encapsulate the essential thrusts of this paper. Things are not always what they seem to be!!! Three are referenced here:

First, the *Austin Chronicle* (Texas) reported that while the "so-called miracle in Texas education got pretty thoroughly probed and sifted during [the 2000 presidential election], yet still no one's sure whether our kids are more proficient at the three Rs, or if standardized tests have dumbed down our expectations. [Politicians have] touted students' rising scores on the TAAS [Texas Assessment of Academic Skills] and national tests as certain indicators of progress, while researchers question whether test results tell the whole story, citing Texas' abysmal high school graduation rate. …When it comes to moving students beyond high school into the college ranks, the state is clearly an underachiever. In late November, a new national study—*'Measuring Up 2000,'* performed by a nonpartisan research group…showed that Texas ranked far behind other states in the percentage of graduates who enroll in and complete college…students' ability to succeed in college is hindered by their lack of participation in high school advanced placement courses that would better prepare them for college-level work. 'Very few students are completing what most people think of as a rigorous college preparatory curriculum…For the class of 1998 …(f)ewer than one in 10 Black graduates met minimal college expectation on the SAT, and only 958 Black students in the entire state reach the top 10 % of their classes. If the state's 35 universities had divided those top-10 graduates equally, each would have added just 27 Black students to its freshman class" (Fullerton, 2000).

Second, the *Sun-Sentinel* (Ft. Lauderdale, Florida) reporting, in part, on the 2000 school year performance with students of African descent as measured by the Florida Comprehensive Assessment Tests observed that with respect to African American learners in…(a different district from the district in which the Florida high school reported on above is located), "students in middle schools scored 5 points higher in reading and 2 points better in mathematics than African Americans across Florida…74 percent of Broward students achieved at least a passing score on the reading test. But that figure for African Americans was 56. In mathematics, 81 percent of all students across the district scored at least a passing score, while only 65 percent of African Americans reached the same score" (Sun Sentinel, 2000, December 24, p. 16B).

Third, Derrick Z. Jackson, a columnist for the Boston Globe cites the NCAA 2000 graduation rates in his article entitled *College Athletes Graduation Gap Bowl*: "The report covers athletes who entered college in either 1990, 1991, 1992, or 1993 and graduated within six years of entrance…there is currently a 17-point percentage gap between the 42 percent national graduation rate of African American players and the 59 percent graduation rate of white players…The worst gaps…Auburn which graduates only 30 percent of African American players to 80 percent of white players. Fresno State (58 to 13), Texas Tech (67 to 23) and Iowa state (67 to 26)" (Sun Sentinel, 2001, January 02, p. 17A).

RECOMMENDATIONS

Analyses such as these, in our view, are critical in order that benchmarking of results of schooling for children and youth of African descent against school performances with white and Asian American students is effected. However, our research and consultation of the literature suggest that benchmarking alone will not result in the desired condition, and suggest that educational leadership must embracing this recommended cyclical process: benchmarking, gap identification, causal analysis, initiative development and funding, and monitoring, in order that *school Improvement* may result from the *reduction of identified gaps to zero*.

CONCLUSION

In the context of the Ellison quote with which we began this chapter, it is recognized that school improvement is *necessary*. Concomitantly, the need to reduce gaps in school performance with African American learners versus categories of students with which the schools have experienced success must be reduced, would that which is both *necessary and possible* be realized.

We elected to end this chapter with a quote from *Saving the African American Child*, a 1984 National Alliance of Black School Educators' report, "Four centuries is a long time to struggle and wait for a quality education. Yet African Americans have done just that. The wait and the struggle continue. Clearly, we as a people are far from our ideal of excellence. We have far greater capacity than opportunities have permitted us to exercise. The expectation of and dependence on quality and excellence in education is a major part of our historical tradition over the millennia. We seek this prize once again" (NABSE, 1984, Page 40). The authors invite leaders at the national, state and local levels to join in the seeking of "this prize" by permitting them to carry out analyses such as those on which they report above for systems or sub-systems over which those leaders have control.

POSTSCRIPT

Critics of this chapter have raised questions framed in terms of "means versus versus ends," and "letting the parents off of the hook." Both issues are related to control-specific paradigms by which specified input and processes are imposed on the parents and educators of other people's children. The authors' responses to these questions, derived from theory that undergirds the zero gap reduction paradigm discussed above, are presented below.

With respect to the means (process) versus ends (product) issue, the authors have observed that whenever there is a serious discussion of school improvement in the context of a zero gap reduction paradigm, the quest for the "solution" or the "silver bullet" or the "perfect" process is inevitably put on the table. This quest, clearly compatible with the color blind and school improvement, exclusively paradigms, narrows the significant question to one of inputs and/or processes. The public policy environment in educational matters is thus relegated to finding or developing narrow, simplistic, often, "one size fits all," and universal process (means) which will, in theory, guarantee the achievement of the desired product (ends). When the ends are the major consideration for policy makers, the means can appropriately be placed with the policy implementers and maintainers. This creates an environment where the ends are clearly defined, codified and validated on the front end, the local flexibility and innovation representing the means are designed to address implementation challenges. In essence, leave the ends to the policy and decision makers, and the means to the implementers and sustainers. Such an arrangement puts flesh on the bones of local control. Equally important, this division makes it possible for construing each classroom as a laboratory in which opportunities for inventing actions and processes by which zero gap reduction may be effected.

The zero gap reduction paradigm suggests four specific school-related roles and functions for parents of African descent: (1) Continue to prepare their children for school in ways consistent with the findings of the Patterson Research Institute [reported above], and effect improvements in indicated areas; (2) Lobby for and insist that their children and youth be schooled in appropriate and desirable educational conditions; (3) Insist that their progeny and the progeny of Arabic, Asian, Hispanic, Native American and white parents be held to the same standards and exposed to the identical curricula; (4) Refuse to permit their children to be tracked, to permit their children to be exposed to lower-level and less rigorous curricula than curricula to which Asian and white children are exposed, refuse to permit the assignment of teachers to teach their children who have not demonstrated effective teacher behavior with learners of African descent, and refuse to permit their children and youth to be placed in inappropriately large classes; and (5) Hold accountable persons who exert control over and who are responsible for systems and sub-systems schooling their children. It goes without saying that a vital and rich resource that should be available to parents of African descent may be found in local and state NABSE Affiliates.

CHAPTER FOUR

THE EDUCATIONAL BRANDING HYPOTHESIS:

Branding African American Learners at an Early Age

A teacher had a very, very successful year... The class results on the yearly achievement test were outstanding, and the special projects the class produced were exceptional. The Principal was very impressed and highly commended the teacher. The teacher thanked the Principal but told him it wasn't very difficult; after all, they were an intellectually gifted class. The Principal knew that the class was not identified as gifted and that the learners had an average academic record. He asked the teacher why she believed they were gifted. She pulled out a piece of paper with the names of her learners; next to the names were numbers such as 139, 143, and so on. When the Principal looked at the paper he realized what she had been referring to. The paper did not give the learners' IQ scores, as the teacher had thought, they gave their locker numbers. The teacher had labeled the learners in that class as gifted. As a result she had very high standards and expectations for what they could and should accomplish, and they did achieve far beyond what others could have expected. I wonder how that class would have done if their locker numbers were in a range of 80 to 100. How would the teacher have labeled them and would her expectations and standards for the class have been lowered?

THE DANGER OF LABELING CHILDREN

BERNARD PERCY, M.A.

EDUCATOR AND AUTHOR

BACKGROUND AND CONTEXT

While the academic success of learners is of paramount importance to parents, teachers and school administrators, the alarming rate of learners with whom schools have failed to effect desired levels of achievement continues to be of concern. Perplexing gaps in school performance with learners of African versus non-African descent, learners from low-income families versus those who are economically privileged, and learners labeled "high achieving" versus "academically challenged" are broad, deep, and persistent. Competing explanations for gaps in school performances with African American versus other learners pervade the literature and include, among others, the inequitable distribution of resources, dismal school leadership, poorly prepared teachers, seemingly inaccessible student services, child rearing practices, and even the nature of learners.

A little noticed study entitled "Student Social Class and Teacher Expectations: The Self-Fulfilling Prophecy in 'Ghetto' Education" (Rist, 1970) suggests an alternative theory by which these gaps may be explained: attribution theory. By this theory, attributes that teachers conceive of and project onto learners, socially defined categories of learners. These socially defined categories are predictive of natures of educational programs to which learners are exposed and extents to which differential measurable outcomes of schooling – gaps in achievement – may be manifested. Rist (1970) suggests a four stage interactional process by which teacher expectations drive outcomes: "(1) the teacher develops expectations regarding certain learners as possessing characteristics or attributes that s/he considers predictive of probable learner futures, (2) the teacher reinforces through his/her mechanisms of differential teacher behavior, previously assigned characteristics or attributes, (3) the learners respond to the attention of the teacher with more of the behavior that initially gained them the assignment of attributes by the teacher, and (4) the teacher takes the responsive behavior of the learners as validation of her original assignment of attributes."

This chapter is prefaced by an episode excerpted from Percy's <u>The Danger of Labeling Children</u>. In the episode Percy's teacher demonstrates the Rist formulation. Because of, or in concert with, the fact that her teacher misconstrued locker numbers as IQ scores she labeled her learners "intellectually gifted," [and] put forth "very high standards and expectations for what they could and should accomplish." Given those expectations, she behaved in such a manner that learner growth was enhanced and encouraged. The learners responded with expected behavior. The teacher took the responsive behavior of the learners as validation of her original assignment perception; her learners were "intellectually gifted."

Of great meaning is the juxtaposition of the principal's belief on the one hand that "the class was not identified as gifted and that the learners had an average academic record" and the evaluative statement that the learners "did achieve far beyond what others could have expected; class results on the yearly achievement test were outstanding, and the special projects the class produced were exceptional," on the other. Percy ends her episode by locating this "belief versus results" phenomenon in the form of the question: "I wonder how that class would have done if their locker numbers were in a range of 80 to 100." The authors find this question both benign and provocative. This is because, as previously shared, it is hypothesized that teachers develop expectations regarding certain learners as possessing characteristics or attributes considered predictive of probable learner futures. The marriage of perceived attributes and predicted probable futures are two pillars upon which rest the practice of branding learners at an early age.

THE NATURE AND SIGNIFICANCE OF LABELING AND BRANDING YOUNG LEARNERS

The two brands at issue here are: "high achieving" and "academically challenged" learners. According to the teachers who responded to our survey, "high achieving" learners are perceived as self—starters, above average, excel in reading, writing, and mathematics, are independent, and take it upon themselves to complete assignments. They are perceived to be independent and disciplined, have good study habits, have strong interpersonal and intrapersonal skills, are learners by nature and have leadership skills. Finally, they are perceived to learn easily, grasp concepts quickly, require little assistance, listen, have a desire to do well, and to be problem solvers. Alternatively, "academically challenged" learners, again according to the teachers who responded to our survey are perceived of as learners who have problems listening and following directions, have short attention spans, limited recall abilities, are easily frustrated, lack understanding, have trouble concentrating, are unable to complete simple tasks, seek negative attention, don't have "discipline," are not prepared for reading mathematics and writing, have no "foundation," suffer from dysfunctional home environments, are not "optimistic" about their educations, and who are disruptive.

When one sees a company's brand on a product, one thinks about the message conveyed – the feelings conjured up in ones mind about that product. The brand name is evocative. The brand name is defining. In the same manner that brand names establish viewpoints about companies or products, the brand names borne by learners, products of processes of formal schooling, cause learners to be likewise affected. Previously shared teacher-provided definitions leave no doubt that differences between learners branded "high achieving" and "academically challenged" are bright, broad and clear. Teachers and other school officials know the differences between the two brands.

Not only are the differences between the two brands known. It appears that surrogates for the brands are salient in the lexicons of African American versus Euro American teachers and other school officials. For example, Gottlieb (1964) reported results of a study of differences in the attitudes of 89 African American and Euro American teachers toward African American learners from low income families. The thirty-six African American and fifty-three Euro American teachers were asked to select from a set of 33 adjectives "those which came closest to describing the children," all of whom were of African descent, "with which the teachers were working." The five items or surrogates for the brands most frequently selected by Euro American versus African American teachers, in the order of frequency, are displayed in Table I.

TABLE I

Surrogates for brands most frequently selected by Euro American versus African American teachers.

	Ethnicities	
Brands	African American	Euro American
(Most frequently selected by Euro American teachers)		
Talkative	06%	59%
Lazy	19%	53%
Fun Loving	74%	45%
High Strung	03%	39%
Rebellious	13%	35%
(Most frequently selected by African American teachers)		
Fun Loving	74%	45%
Happy	65%	31%
Cooperative	61%	35%
Energetic	49%	33%
Ambitious	36%	20%

Surrogates for brands least frequently selected by Euro American and African American teachers are displayed in Table II:

TABLE II

Surrogates for brands most frequently selected by Euro American versus African American teachers.

	Ethnicities	
Brands	African American	Euro American
Cultured	10%	02%
Idealistic	10%	06%
Intellectual	03%	02%
Methodical	06%	00%
Poised	06%	06%
Sophisticated	03%	00%
Witty	08%	00%

It appears to also be the case that learners are not branded as "high achieving" and "academically challenged" serendipitously, by chance or by accident. Hatch (2002) suggests that branding "actually occurs somewhere between the vision of top management for the brand and its future, the organizational culture that supports the brand promise, and the images held by key stakeholders that forge the reputation as well as inform the branding process." Later Hatch restates this formulation with "the brand results from the alignment between the strategic vision of top management, the organizational culture that emerges from the everyday life in the organization, and the images that stakeholders hold and share of the product."

Farmer (2002) approaches branding from a somewhat different but related perspective. Branding, he writes, "is nothing more than a series of associations in the consumer's mind that influence their propensity to prefer …a product over its competitors…These associations" Farmer goes on "can include brand knowledge ('facts'…), brand image ('symbolic associations'…), and brand emotion (the overall 'feeling' that the consumer has for the brand)." Farmer stipulates that in order to "elevate" ones product to a brand one must develop the types of associations that one wants ones brand to have. Thus, the brand is bestowed by design and is a creature of the coexistence of the vision held for the learner by those who have the power and authority to make decisions about the education of the learner; the culture of the school or the rules and regulation that govern the behavior of school role incumbents such as counselors, teachers and administrators; and how stakeholders think about and value the learner.

These antecedents to the brand come together in the kindergarten observed by Rist (1970) who reported that based on four sources of information, the kindergarteners were placed in permanent groups, "those expected to learn and those expected not to permeate the teacher's orientation to the class," on the eighth day of kindergarten. First: a pre-registration form completed by mothers of the children entering the kindergarten class. What turned out to be important information provided was whether the entering learners "had had any pre-school experience." Second: the school social worker supplied a list of all enrolling learners who "lived in homes that received public welfare funds." Third: interviews of mothers during which medical information, as well as specific "parental concerns" such as "thumb-sucking, bed-wetting, loss of bowel control, lying, stealing, fighting, and laziness" were elicited. Finally, the teacher's prior experience and the experience of other teachers with learners' siblings translated into information about the probable behavioral and academic performances of the entering kindergarten learners. Assignment to these groups on the eighth day of kindergarten turned out to be tantamount to the beginning of a life sentence as by second grade, little or no change in the composition of the groups were evident. Rist observed that none of the information used as bases for the educational decisions made "related directly to the academic potential of the incoming kindergarten child."

THE PROBLEM

Relationships between and among ways in which learners are perceived, categorized, labeled and branded; differential educational programs to which branded learners are exposed; resulting differential outcomes of instruction, and the utilization of outcome data to reinforce initial perceptions and rationales for branding learners have previously been discussed. Additionally, we learn from *The Hindu,* India's online National Newspaper, that these relationships are not confined to national borders - "According to some reports, the Central Board of Secondary Education is toying with the idea of assigning grades A, B, C,D, and E for the performance of the learners in the forthcoming examination…." The writer goes on with "this amounts to labeling and branding the child for life…This may lead to a disastrous consequence…" (Hubli, 2002).

Relatedly, the authors discovered through research a memorandum of understanding between the Karnataka Government, Karnataka is a State in Southern India, and a local Foundation, which ensures "education for every child in the State, universal education for all." The first principal…: "all children, irrespective of gender, caste, community or religion, come to school with substantial pre-knowledge and have infinite capacity to learn. No steps or measures will be taken that will undermine their self-esteem and self-confidence by labeling them as failures or branding them as incapable of learning and giving up on them…" (Memorandum of Understanding, 2001).

Self esteem! Self-confidence! Labeling! and Branding. We learn from PublicChristian.com that George Bush, after reviewing a house in West Africa from which slaves were shackled and shipped to America, stated "Human beings were delivered, sorted, weighed, branded with marks of commercial enterprises and loaded as cargo on a voyage without return." Dorothy Allison echoed this reality in her novel entitled <u>Bastard out of Carolina</u>. In a paper written by an unknown author, Allison's portrayal of the struggle with identity of a young poor white girl named "Bone" is discussed. The writer of the article observes, "Allison uses metaphors and degrading diction to illustrate how society imposes class stereotypes onto identity to dehumanize and diminish the value of an individual." Bone's mother is consumed by the fact that Bone's birth certificate lacked a stamp on it – thus designating Bone a "bastard." According to the author of the article "Allison uses 'stamp on the birth certificate' as a physical parallel to the social 'stamp' or stigma that society prints to label and then sort individuals as objects into classes." Allison also uses a metaphor, again according to the anonymous writer, "to describe the 'stamp' with 'burned' to imply a branding process that dehumanizes the individual by creating a painful and permanent identifying mark and treating the individual like a cow or other such animal…Allison specifically [locates the story in] 'Greenville County' to provide a societal institution, part of the government, that forces class structure labels. Also by using 'County,' Allison emphasizes the individual versus the institution that attempts to 'name' her and diminish her value as an individual" (Unknown, 2003).

Clearly, then, the branding of learners at an early age is perceived by some to be an institutional problem. What are less clear are the points in time at which learners of African descent first experience the burn of the brand, how and to what extent learners of African descent are branded, how and to what extent African American versus Non-African American teachers brand learners of African descent, and the specific nature of the brands. Previously we cited George Bush's use of the phrase "branded with marks of commercial enterprises." In the same PublicChristian.com document in which the George Bush quote appeared, the following question is raised: "'Branded.' Is anything like that happening today?" That question was seminal to the area of inquiry pursued in this study.

PROCESS AND OUTCOMES

In this chapter the authors seek to explain the inability of the school to reduce the achievement gap to zero by educating all learners with equity in such a way that the schools effect equal outcomes of schooling for African American and non-African American learners. The explanation at issue in this research report known as the <u>Educational Branding Hypothesis</u> anticipates the first stage of the Rist formulation (the teacher develops expectations regarding certain learners as possessing characteristics or attributes that she considers predictive of probable learner futures) by answering the following set of questions specific to the branding of learners as "high achieving" versus "academically challenged" learners and sorting learners into categories of learners perceived by classroom teachers and other school officials to possess differential characteristics or attributes.

In order to shed light on aspects of the Educational Branding Hypothesis the authors sought to answer the following questions:

I. Do teachers label or brand learners and if so at which educational level does this practice begin?

II. Do teachers label or brand African American vs. non-African American learners differentially?

III. Do African American vs. non-African American teachers label or brand African American learners differentially?

IV. Do African American and non African American teachers project identical attributes onto African American learners?

TABLE III
Ethnicities of Teachers Responding to our Survey

Ethnicities							
African American		Hispanic		White		Other	
N	**%**	**N**	**%**	**N**	**%**	**N**	**%**
22	56	4	10	12	31	1	3

A survey instrument that included several germane questions was self-administered by 22 African American and 17 non-African American teachers. Ethnicities of the teachers who responded to our survey are displayed in Table III. Each responding teacher was asked to identify six "high achieving" and six "academically challenged" learners, assign six adjectives or surrogates for the brands to each identified learner, share their own and the gender and ethnicity and the six identified students, along with other pertinent information. Reported information was entered to a spreadsheet, using Microsoft Excel, and analyzed in a manner appropriate to our research question. This process yielded a sample of 174 learners. Student ethnicities and brands of teacher-identified learners are displayed in Table IV.

TABLE IV
Ethnicities of Teachers Responding to our Survey

Brands	Ethnicities							
	African American		Hispanic		White		Other	
	N	%	N	%	N	%	N	%
"High Achieving"	73	65	29	26	10	9	1	<1
"Acad. Challenged"	36	59	17	28	8	13	0	0

QUESTION I

Question I was: "Do teachers label or brand learners and if so at which educational level does this practice begin?" As previously reported, Rist (1970) found that learners were labeled, and placed in permanent groups or categories by the eighth day of Kindergarten. Thirty years later, provision of education at the Pre-Kindergarten level is prevalent. Our hunch, however, was that the branding of learners would not commence at a point in time earlier than Kindergarten. We found that that our hunch was not supported by the data. Branding of learners by those who responded to our survey did in fact commence in Pre-Kindergarten. In Table V the distribution of the learners taught by those who responded to our survey by grade levels is displayed. It may be seen from Table V that fifteen percent of the learners in both brands were so branded in Pre-Kindergarten or Kindergarten. Thus it is evident that the teachers who responded to our survey do brand learners and that this branding begins in Pre-kindergarten.

TABLE V
The Distribution of respondents by Grade Levels and Brands

Brand	Grade Levels															
	Pre-K		K		1		2		3		4		5		6	
	N	%	N	%	N	%	N	%	N	%	N	%	N	%	N	%
"High Achieving"	2	2	15	13	9	8	15	13	27	24	30	26	12	11	3	3
"Acad. Chal"	6	10	3	5	7	12	9	15	15	25	8	13	9	15	4	7

QUESTION II

Question II was "Do teachers label or brand African American vs. non-African American learners differentially? Participating teacher assigned 294 and 457 labels to learners branded as "High Achieving" and "Academically

Challenged" learners, respectively. Categories and mean frequencies of labels assigned are displayed in Table VI. High-frequency labels or surrogates for the brands assigned to African American v. Non-African American learners were designated twice as frequently than the mean; 3.12 ("High Achieving" and 3.22 "Academically Challenged" learners). Surrogates for the brands assigned by brand are displayed in Table VII.

TABLE VI

The Numbers, Categories and Mean Frequencies of Assigned Labels by Brands

Brand	Numbers of Labels	Numbers of Categories	Mean Frequencies of Labels
"High Achieving"	294	188	1.56
"Academically Challenged"	457	204	2.24

It may be seen from the top third of the Table VII (page 94) distribution that African Americans branded "High Achieving" learners were labeled: "Smart," and "Friendly." Non-African Americans branded as 'High Achieving" learners were labeled: "Smart," "Bright," "Quiet," "Respectful," "Creative," and "Helper." African Americans branded as "Academically Challenged" learners were labeled: "Leader," "Playful," and "Smart." Non-African American branded as 'Academically Challenged" learners "Quiet," "Frustrated," "Slow," "Friendly," and "Leader."

Given these findings, the question must be answered in the affirmative. While learners of African Descent branded as "High Achieving" were labeled "Smart" and "Friendly," they were not perceived as "Bright," "Respectful," or "Creative" as were their counter-part Non-African American learners. Further, labels in the top third of the distribution assigned to African American learners branded as "High Achieving" ("Smart" and "Friendly") do not seem meaningfully different from those assigned to African American learners branded as "Academically Challenged" ("Leader," "Playful," and "Smart"). It may be seen by inspection that this was not the case with Non-African American learners. Finally, the fact that more than two-thirds of the attributes in the top third of the distribution were assigned to Non-African American learners did not escape the notice of the researchers.

TABLE VII

Labels or Surrogates for the Brands Assigned to African American V. Non-African American Learners by Brand and Frequencies in Percentages

African American Learners				Non-African American Learners			
"High Achieving"		"Acad. Challenged"		"High Achieving"		"Acad. Challenged"	
				Smart	11.4		
Smart	10.2						
		Leader	9.4			Quiet	8.7
				Bright	6.3	Frustrated	6.8
				Quiet	6.3	Slow	6.8
Friendly	5.0	Playful	5.4	Respectful	5.0	Friendly	5.8
		Smart	5.4	Creative	5.0	Leader	5.8
				Helper	5.0		
Hard Wrkg	4.6	Bright	4.7			Shy	4.9
Talkative	4.6	Slow	4.7				
		Happy	4.0				
		Motivator	4.0				
		Outgoing	4.0				
		Quiet	4.0				
		Talkative	4.0				
Active	3.7	Hrd Workg	3.36	Conscntious	3.8	Creative	3.8
Friendly	3.7	Unfocused	3.36	Energetic	3.8	Energetic	3.8
Outgoing	3.7			Polite	3.8		
				Shy	3.8		
				Talkative	3.8		
		Angry	2.68				
		Athletic	2.68				
		Attitude	2.68				
		Energetic	2.68				
		Sneaky	2.68				

QUESTION III

Question III was "Do African American vs. non-African American teachers label or brand African American learners differentially?" It was seen from Table IV that African American teachers who responded to our survey more often branded learners as 'High Achieving" than they branded learners as "Academically Challenged." Hispanic teachers who responded to our survey seemed to brand learners equally as "High Achieving" and "Academically Challenged." Euro-American teachers who responded to our survey more often branded learners as "Academically Challenged" than "High Achieving."

From Table VIII it is seen that labels most frequently used (the top third of the distribution) neither appreciatively differentiate between African American and Non-African American teachers nor between learners branded as "High Achieving" and "Academically Challenged." It is noted, however, that all labels in the bottom half of the distribution are associated by the African American and Non-African American teachers who re-

TABLE VIII

Labels assigned by African American V. Non-African American Teachers to Learner of African Descent Branded as 'High Achieving" and "Academically Challenged."

African Americans Teachers				Non African American Teachers			
"High Achieving"		"Acad. Challenged"		"High Achieving"		"Acad. Challenged"	
Smart	12.2						
		Leader	10.7				
Talkative	6.8	Bright	6.7				
Active	5.4			Bright	5.7		
Friendly	5.4			Energetic	5.7		
Happy	4.1	Playful	4.9			Smart	4.9
Hard Worker	4.1						
Sweet	4.1						
		Motivator	3.9	Athletic	3.8	Happy	3.7
		Outgoing	3.9	Hard Worker	3.8	Leader	3.7
		Quiet	3.9	Kind	3.8	Shy	3.7
		Slow	3.9	Motivated	3.8	Slow	3.7
		Smart	3.9	Neat	3.8		
		Talkative	3.9	Outgoing	3.8		
				Polite	3.8		
				Smart	3.8		
Awesome	2.7	Active	2.9			Attitude	2.4
Bossy	2.7	Angry	2.9			Disrespectful	2.4
Cooperative	2.7	Alert	2.9			Distracted	2.4
Girlish	2.7	Athletic	2.9			Forgetful	2.4
Outgoing	2.7	Energetic	2.9			Frustrated	2.4
Playful	2.7	Hard Worker	2.9			Hard Worker	2.4
Pretty	2.7	Hyper	2.9			Helper	2.4
Responsible	2.7	Impatient	2.9			Immature	2.4
Sensitive	2.7	Sensitive	2.9			Inc. Work	2.4
Shy	2.7					Insecure	2.4
						Motivator	2.4
						Over Bearing	2.4
						Playful	2.4
						Punctual	2.4
		Attitude	1.9			Quiet	2.4
		Explorer	1.9			Sneaky	2.4
		Follower	1.9			Struggling	2.4
		Friendly	1.9			Sweet	2.4
		Happy	1.9			Unfocused	2.4
		Impulsive	1.9				
		Lazy	1.9				
		Loud	1.9				
		Optimistic	1.9				
		Outspoken	1.9				
		Seeking	1.9				
		Shy	1.9				
		Sneaky	1.9				
		Spoiled	1.9				

sponded to our survey with learners branded as "Academically Challenged." Given our analysis, we must conclude that the African American and non-African American teachers who responded to our survey do not label or brand African American learners, differentially.

QUESTION IV

Question IV was "Do African American and non African American teachers identify identical attributes of African American learners? In order to answer this question, the authors arrayed all attributes reported by the African American and Non-African American teachers who responded to our survey. Percentages of times African American and Non-African American teachers assigned each label were computed and arrayed in Table IX.

From Table IX it is seen that the African American and non-African American teachers who responded to our survey are in agreement with respect to the labels that appear in the bottom half of the distribution. This finding supports, in part, our response to Question III: "Do African American vs. non-African American teachers label or brand African American learners, differentially?" However, some would argue that with respect to the labels most often assigned, those in the top half of the distribution, meaningful differences in attributes assigned by African American versus non African American teachers are found. Some positive labels such as "Leader," "Motivator," "Attentive," and "Smart," are more often assigned by African American teachers. However, they also more frequently assign "Slow," "Sneaky," and "Talkative." Non- African American teachers more frequently assigned negative labels such as "Immature," and "insecure."

Regarding our question, "Do African American and non African American teachers project identical attributes onto African American learners," as already noted, respondents were in agreement with respect to the infrequently assigned labels that appear in the bottom half of the distribution on Table IX. With respect to labels most often assigned, those in the top third of the distribution, meaningful differences in attributes assigned by African American versus non African American teachers were found.

CONCLUSION

In this report we have attempted to shed light on the practice of branding

TABLE IX

Comparisons of Labels assigned by African American V. Non-African American Teachers to Learner of African Descent in Percentages.

Labels	African Americans Teachers	Non African American Teachers	Percent Difference
Leader	12.5	5.0	7.5
Energetic	7.5	2.5	5.0
Motivator	7.5	2.5	5.0
Quiet	7.5	2.5	5.0
Athletic	5.0	2.5	2.5
Attentive	5.0	2.5	2.5
Helper	2.5	5.0	2.5
Immature	2.5	5.0	2.5
Insecure	2.5	5.0	2.5
Over Achiever	2.5	5.0	2.5
Slow	7.5	5.0	2.5
Smart	7.5	5.0	2.5
Sneaky	5.0	2.5	2.5
Talkative	7.5	5.0	2.5
Angry	2.5	2.5	0.0
Happy	5.0	5.0	0.0
Hardworking	5.0	5.0	0.0
Over Whelming	2.5	2.5	0.0
Playful	5.0	5.0	0.0
Pleasant	2.5	2.5	0.0
Pre-occupied	2.5	2.5	0.0
Respectful	2.5	2.5	0.0
Self Confident	2.5	2.5	0.0
Shy	5.0	5.0	0.0
Stubborn	2.5	2.5	0.0
Sweet	2.5	2.5	0.0
Unfocused	2.5	2.5	0.0
Unmotivated	2.5	2.5	0.0

learners at an early age. Our finding that branding begins in Pre-Kindergarten, is particularly distasteful, as once branded, the educational programs to which learners are exposed and associated outcomes of schooling are defined and durable. With that reality in mind, we thought that we would close with the following quote from *Saving the African American Child*, A Report of the National Alliance of School Educators:

Not all teachers fail to achieve excellence with African American students. This simple fact seems not to be understood by many teacher educators. Low income, poor nutrition, non-common language variation, etc. *are not the causes of low performance for students!* These things may determine what treatment students get from educators. The *treatment* that they get determines success or failure (p.27).

CHAPTER FIVE

REFLECTIONS ON *CULTURAL AND EDUCATIONAL EXCELLENCE REVISITED*

Issues associated with the quality, equity, and efficiency required to save the African American child can be connected from the 1896 Plessy case to the 1954 Brown case of today. The exercise of examining and articulating cultural and educational issues related to *Saving the African American Child* have inspired our thoughtful reflections and caused us to project towards the future. With this in mind we share our final thoughts.

This text flows from general information to specific issues in a series of ongoing cycles. First, social progress was examined, second school performance was studied and lastly, learners were targeted. Our ultimate purpose is to provide relevant data towards the promotion or betterment of the African American child. The following graph depicts the aforementioned cycles:

System	Social Progress (Ch. 2)
↕	
Sub-system	School Performance/Gap Identification (Ch. 3)
↕	↕
Group (Individual)	African American Learners (Ch. 4)

Students are not just students. They are brothers and sisters, nieces and nephews, sons and daughters, and the list could continue. Even as children, we learn to adapt to several roles within our lives. In knowing that, we must come to view our children holistically in order that we might understand and recognize the many needs of our African American children. Holistically speaking, we must view the child as one person who is adapting or attempting to adapt in many cases to various roles in society. Hence, it is important to note that society is constantly changing, everything from the structure of the family to the labor market. With change comes a set of different demands. For example, with the changing structure of the family, the state of the labor market, changing economic demands and labor market demands, everyone is experiencing some type of effect.

No one is exempt from experiencing the effects of a rapidly changing economy. Perhaps our children are most impacted and the least likely to receive attention in light of how things are changing. Perhaps they are not equipped to deal with change adequately. And how could we expect them to thrive when things are constantly changing when they may or may not be fully equipped to cope with change? The constantly changing conditions of our society are having negative impacts in the labor market, on social demands and economic demands, to name a few. Therefore, it is for this reason that we prescribe to utilizing Maslow's Hierarchy of Needs. From an educator's standpoint, the indication here is that basic needs must be met before learning can transpire. For example, if a child is not eating at home, how can we expect him/her to function on any level when all he/she can think about is his/her next meal?

We cannot separate the child into parts and deal with one part of him/her while at school and ignore the other situations that may have impacted him at home (role of son) or on his way to school (role of friend). We must deal with the child from a holistic point of view. It is in meeting the basic needs and educational needs of the child that we can begin to build and encourage him/her to develop a positive self concept. In developing a child's self-concept, we will see the after effects of a positive self-concept in his or her cultural and academic excellence. As mentioned earlier within the text, academic excellence cannot be reached without cultural excellence. Cultural excellence is embedded in an individual's self-esteem, self-concept, self-knowledge, self-awareness, and self-actualization. Self-esteem relates to how one feels about oneself. Self-concept involves one's view of oneself. Self-knowledge is knowing oneself and self-awareness is being aware of who one is. Self-actualization is the manifestation of a certain level of congruence between one's feelings of oneself, one's view of oneself, and knowing and being aware of whom one is. To become self-actualized is a sign of growth to a point of truly understanding and knowing oneself where one exhibits such growth in one's decisions, accomplishments, actions and reactions in day-to-day life.

In order to achieve self-actualization, which would ultimately lead to academic excellence, we compared the African American child to a flower. For example, what is a flower? A flower is a living thing that has a stem, petals, and life. Would it still be a flower without a stem or without petals? No, it would be a dead flower. Therefore, in analyzing or comparing our African American children to flowers, the stem would be self-esteem and self-concept, and the petals on the bloom with petals of self-awareness and self-knowledge, one should envision flower would be self knowledge and self awareness. When the flower is in full self-actualization. Self-actualization could be transferred towards the development of cultural excellence and subsequently to academic excellence. The following diagram is an illustration of the context of this text in terms of the African American learner achieving cultural and educational excellence:

Social Progress	System	Social Progress (Ch. 2)
⇕	⇕	⇕
Academic Excellence	Sub-system	School Performance/ Gap Identification (Ch. 3)
⇕	⇕	⇕
Cultural Excellence	Group (Individual)	African American Learners (Ch. 4)
⇕		
Self-actualization		
⇕		
Self-concept Self –esteem		

So now you may wonder, where and when do we begin and what should we do? The two-fold answer is that we must begin right here and right now and we should begin by fostering the development of the self esteem and self concept of our African American children. Building self esteem and self concept has everything to do with an image or images. As the entertainer Whitney Houston sang "I believe the children are our future, teach them well and let them lead the way, show them all the beauty they possess inside. Give them a sense of pride, to make it easier….". If we begin to nurture our African American children and provide them with positive images of things, individuals or places that resemble what they look like and what they may have a desire to do or become then we are beginning the process of developing the child's self esteem and self concept. We have a few things we must do for our children: We have to **B**uild, **L**ove, **E**mbrace, **N**urture, **D**irect and **D**ivulge (B.L.E.N.D.) our African American children today. We have to build the self concept and self esteem of our African American children with love. We have to embrace and nurture them in order to build them up. But in the process, for them, we must also direct and divulge. If we use **B.L.E.N.D**. as a guide, we are sure to make a difference in the lives of our African American children today as well as impact their future. We must not forget that the African American children of today, will soon be the leaders of tomorrow. We must feel a certain level of indebtedness to them so that we could ensure that we influence them now to become strong, confident leaders, caregivers, husbands, wives, mothers and fathers. Our children are our future, let us all make a contribution to the betterment of our African American children.

S<small>LB</small>

2005

H<small>OUSTON</small>, T<small>EXAS</small>

Upon close examination, the contents of the chapters causes one to step back from the realities evident in the academic results that are distinguishable by race, class, school environment, and neighborhood wealth to be able to visualize appropriate strategies and tactics for transforming educational institutions to meet the needs of a diverse student population. It has been demonstrated that despite continuing achievement gaps, questionable labeling practices, and unethical as well as ineffective teaching practices, some children of color from low income families have managed to meet or exceed rigorous academic standards on a consistent basis. Thus my reflections are directed at those students who excel under challenging circumstances so that the compelling evidence is so overwhelming that the slogans of "All Children Can Learn" and "No Child Left Behind" will enable the development and implementation of policies and practices that produce enhanced academic achievement.

A recent account of the importance of high expectations and challenging course involvement revealed:

> "The rigor of the academic coursework that a student takes in high school is a better predictor of whether that student will graduate from college than test scores, grade point average, or class rank. This correlation is even stronger for African-American and Latino students and is very significant for low-income students."
>
> (Tirozzi, June 2004)

These factors are critical to effective schools and successful students and well within the control of local school officials. Yet indictments continue to be leveled leveled against educators whose behavior and attitudes have not allowed them to adapt their instruction to the strengths of the learners in far too many classrooms. Wimberly (2002) addressed the critical nature of relationships as a variable that must be addressed in closing the academic achievement gap:

> "A strong relationship with a teacher, counselor or administrator in high school can help propel students to college or other post-secondary education. However, research shows that African American students are less likely than their white peers to develop the type of bond with an adult at school that facilitates college-going."

The attitudinal barriers imposed on students by teachers who unknowingly, in some cases, depressed the aspirations of some learners of African descent can be viewed as a significant challenge that must be met with appropriate responses by those who carry the opportunities connected to educational leadership. Jerald (2001) cites an Education Trust report that "provides a state-by-state and national analysis of high-poverty and high-minority schools nationwide that scored in the top one-third of all schools. These schools often out-performed predominantly white schools in wealthy communities."

The importance of school effects has been the major focus of the "Effectiveness" research pioneered by the late Ron Edmonds in his work with schools in New York that resulted in characteristics being identified and disseminated that have influenced both educational policies and practices. Ferguson (2002) indicated that racial disparities in high-achieving suburban schools could be addressed if "schools, communities, and state and federal policymakers: 1) assume no motivation differences, 2) address specific skill deficits, 3) supply ample encouragement routinely, and 4) provide access to resources and learning experiences."

However, the empirical data necessary to fortify contentions about effectiveness suffers, from our perspective, because the range that separates high achieving learners of African descent from those who meet minimum expectations on measures of academic achievement remains unexplored fully. The extent to which the characteristics existed and factors are realized has not been examined against their impact on different results between high performing and minimal performing learners of African descent adequately in a variety of school settings. For example, Fordham (2001) posited that "the conflict experienced by academically successful and unsuccessful students in a predominantly Black high school in Washington, D.C. is premised on their experiencing inordinate ambivalence and affective dissonance around the issue of academic excellence in the school context." One might readily conclude that unless there are appropriate interventions to prevent the view of academic academically successful and unsuccessful Black students. Other authors have discussed what shall be termed the "aura of achievement" as a critical achievement as "acting white," the spillover effect will depress the amount of energy, commitment, and time devoted to academic preparation by both component that separates high performing from minimal performing learners of African descent. Collectively, the authors of this book have analyzed and applied information related to Carter's (2002) assertion that effective educators must **understand that "African Americans' psychological orientations to their racial** identity and cultural values, as well as socio- political circumstances, are the context within which African American educational success should be assessed and formulated."

The vital role that teacher quality plays in the success of students and the effectiveness of schools as well as communities has been a focus of the gap reduction strategies and tactics advocated. This coupled with the standards-based reform efforts championed at the federal and state levels of educational governance as well as the demands for productive and visionary leadership are part of the problem solving scenario. Ferguson (2002) offers some insights gleaned from a survey of secondary school students in high performing suburban school districts that should prove instructive in the teacher quality dialogue related to high performing learners of African descent.

"1. Assume no motivational differences.

It seems likely that incorrect assumptions about group differences in effort and interest may lead some schools to under invest in searching for ways to raise achievement levels among African-Americans, Hispanics, and some mixed race students. Teachers should assume that there are no systematic, group-level differences in effort or motivation to succeed, even when there are clearly observable differences in behavior and academic performance.

and

2. Supply ample encouragement routinely.

Given the importance that African American and Hispanic students assign to teacher encouragement, teachers need to be aware of what students regard as encouraging. Using this awareness, they need to provide effective forms of encouragement routinely. This encouragement should be matched with truly effective instruction and other forms of academic support both inside and outside the classroom."

The pathways to excellence, equity, and legitimacy in institutions of learning have been scrutinized so that the journeys to a destination where all students can be successful, all teachers can embrace student strengths through quality instruction, and all educational leaders can provide effective learning environments have been explored and charted. Therefore, the next steps for those who would learn, teach, and lead is to answer the interrogatives that follows:

If not now, when? If not us, who?

JRC

2005

HOUSTON, TEXAS

"I'm amazed when people actually plant onions and then go out later and hope to harvest tomatoes. Wait a minute. If you're not even religious, nature has shown us for millions of years if you get anything back, it will be millions of what you planted. So that's why back to your question, what do we—what has happened in the 50 years (since the Brown vs. Board of Education] decision). If we don't plant the right things, we will reap the wrong things. It goes without saying. And . . . you don't have [to have] an I.Q. Of 150. Just common sense tells you to be kind, ninny. Fool, be kind."

Dr. Maya Angelou during an interview with Tavis Smiley

Thursday May 20, 2004

In my view, two meaningful events occurred during the course of my contributing to *Cultural and Educational Excellence Revisited*. A first such event involved comments made by Dr. Bill Cosby the Entertainer, (shades of Cedric the Entertainer) during a National Association for the Advancement of Colored People (NAACP) ceremony commemorating the 50th anniversary of the Brown v. Board of Education Supreme Court decision outlawing "separate but equal" schools. A second meaningful event was the death of Ray Charles.

Upon reflection, these two events caused me to renew my focus on salient aspects of a previously cited letter written by Dr. Don Smith, former President of the National Alliance of Black School Educators that introduced the Saving the African American Child report. Recall from Chapter One of *Cultural and Educational Excellence Revisited* that Dr. Smith presented *Saving the African American Child*, as a "philosophical statement of belief and expectation" and shared that "while our single objective is to save African American children, we believe that all American children will be better served by an educational system which is based on the goals of academic and cultural excellence as defined in this report." If "all American children will be better served by an educational system which is based on the goals of academic and cultural excellence," it certainly would be the case for all American children of African descent.

Dr. Cosby the Entertainer's remarks were made at Washington's historic Constitution Hall during a celebration of the 1954 Supreme Court decision that marked the beginning of the end of racial segregation in many of America's "separate but equal" institutions. While Dr. Cosby the Entertainer's remarks were far ranging, a fair summary would be that he blamed African Americans from low income families for their economic status, for what Frazier labeled "conspicuous consumption," for the incarceration of children and youth of African descent by the criminal "injustice" system, for the teaching of "poor" English to children of African descent by their parents, and for being endowed with Afrocentric names.

Kiah Thomas, a 13 year old student in the San Francisco Bay area responding to Dr. Cosby the Entertainer's Afrocentric names observation wrote: "…with names like Shaniqua, Taliqua and Mohammed and all of that crap…" with "…you may think my name is 'crap,' but it actually means "season's beginning in Kiswahili. I was born on December 20, the end of fall and the beginning of winter…Some of my friend's names are Shameka, Makeeba, Shaquana and Kashia, and none of us are in jail…When I read the remarks you made, I wondered whether Shaniqua was sitting in the audience that night, and what she felt when she heard you mention her name. I wonder if she went to school the next day feeling proud to have been able to attend a gala event to celebrate an historic occasion like the 50th Anniversary of Brown v. Board of Education, whether she felt like she had been kicked in the stomach, or whether she just blew off the whole thing as just another old man talking too much" (San Francisco Bay View, 2004). I wonder how Barack Obama, potentially the third American of African descent to sit in the United States Senate since Reconstruction, felt about Dr. Cosby the Entertainer's "Afrocentric names" observation.

Dr. Michael Eric Dyson, a professor of religious studies and African studies at the University of Pennsylvania, characterized Dr. Cosby the Entertainer's remarks as statements that "betray classist, elitist viewpoints that are rooted in generational warfare." Dr. Dyson went on to observe that Dr. Cosby the Entertainer was "ill-informed on the critical and complex issues that shape people's lives" (Tavis Smily Show, May 27, 2004). Dr. Dyson is quoted elsewhere as having said, "a better use of the platform would have been to criticize national public policy for failing to give poor people enough support" (Tennant, 2004).

Reporting on the death, eulogy, and interment of Ray Charles caused me to, again focus on the conditions, treatment received by, and outcomes for learners of African descent from low income families, learners who are disabled, and learners who may have been "pushed out" of school. Ray Charles lost his sight during his childhood and left school at a relatively early age. It is in some ways ironic, given Dr. Cosby the Entertainer's remarks on a NAACP platform, that "[o]ne of Ray Charles' last public appearances was at the NAACP Image Awards "in March, when he was inducted into the Association's hall of Fame" (Clark, 2004). This is the same Ray Charles who gave us "Tell your mama, tell your pa, I'm gonna send you back to Arkansas," "Talkin 'bout You," and "what'd I Say" - language that overlaps the derisive observations about the speech of some African Americans made by Dr. Cosby the Entertainer.

In the same previously cited Tavis Smily interview, Dr. Angelou went on to make the following comment: "Somehow we really think that, 'I'm separate from you.' 'He's different from me.' 'I don't like them.' "'My people never liked them.' 'They are gay.' 'They are [B]lack.' 'They are white.' 'They are fat.' 'They are thin.' That is so stupid. It is so blitheringly stupid, and it—Unfortunately, it is an epidemic of ignorance which has assailed us all over the world" (Dr. Maya Angelou. Interview with Tavis Smiley, Thursday, May 20, 2004). Her thought taken in the context of careful discernment and consideration of the Bill Cosby and Ray Charles "events" have rendered me committed to the provision of better outcomes of schooling, in Dr. Smith's words, "for all learners," especially for all learners of African descent.

While my use of the term "all learners of African descent" refers to – all learners rooted in Africa, without regard to height, weight, gender, place of birth, language, religion, skin color, parentage, sexual preference, class or caste, or physical or mental disability, I came to focus on specific segments of learners of African descent in the course of contributing to *Cultural and Educational Excellence Revisited* - learners who have migrated to the United States from the Caribbean and learners who have migrated to the United States from Africa. I do not seek to suggest this to be a novel focus or that the American born learner of African descent was the exclusive interest of the *Saving the African American Child* authors. To the contrary!!!

However, as a result of discernment and research it has become, in my view, increasingly apparent that the extent to which we fail to embrace "all learners of African descent," including learners in these two populations, is the extent to which we may find saving American born learners of African descent increasingly beyond our collective grasp. I have reached this conclusion in view of the following:

o   Immigrant Blacks have largely been ignored, both in discussions about racial discrimination and about the assimilation of immigrants (Butcher, 1900).

o   According to an analysis of Census Bureau data carried out by the State University of New York, "the population of Blacks from Africa and the Caribbean grew roughly seven times as fast" as American born Blacks Between 1980 and 2000 (Armas, 2004). (Takougang (Undated) states that the "influx of African immigrants to the United States in the last two decades has been phenomenal. According to figures from the Immigration and Naturalization Services (INS), the number of African immigrants to the United states more than quadrupled in the last two decades [1981-2000]").

o   "The number of Blacks who arrived from or claimed ancestry to nations in the Caribbean or West Indies, such as Jamaica or Haiti, more than tripled between 1980 and 2000" (Armas, 2004).

o "The median household income for Blacks from the Caribbean or Africa is about $40,000, nearly $7,000 more than for African Americans," (Armas, 2004). See also (Takougang (Undated). According to Sowell, "…immigrants from the West Indies…do very well compared to native-born Blacks. Not only are their incomes higher, but in a myriad of other socioeconomic characteristics (fertility, education, crime rates) the West Indian immigrants…perform better" (In Butcher, 1990).

o Only 5% of African immigrants now residing in Harris county [Houston] have no more than high school diplomas (this compares with 12.8 percent of American–born Blacks); 62% have college degrees (50.5 % for American born Blacks) and 35% have post –graduate credentials" (8.4 % for American –born Blacks) " 'Remarkably" according to Klineberg, "the newcomers from Africa (primarily Nigeria) have higher levels of education than any other immigrant community interviewed in the survey, including Asians" (Klineberg, 2002). Nationally, according to Butcher (1990), African immigrants "…have completed 15.7 years of schooling, or the equivalent of 3.7 years of college… A higher percentage of the Africans are college graduates and have attended some graduate school (53.3%) than any other group, including the white natives and white immigrants."

o "African immigrants to the United States no longer come only from former English-speaking colonies – as had been the case for decades since those from none English-speaking colonies often found it difficult to learn a new language – but include immigrants from former Portuguese, Spanish and French colonies (Takougang, Undated).

o "The unemployment rate of 10 percent for [American-born Blacks] in 2000 was about 3 percentage points higher than for Caribbean-born Blacks and 5 percentage points higher than for Blacks from Africa] (Armas, 2004).

o Immigrant Black men live nine years longer than native –born Black men…according to an analysis by a National Institutes of Health researcher" (Pritchard, 2004). While "The average [native]-born Black man could expect to reach 64, while [an immigrant] Black man... would likely live beyond 73,...An African–born man remaining in his homeland might well die before his 50th birthday" (Pritchard, 2004).

Thus the question must be raised as to how one accounts for the quality of life apparently enjoyed by Black Immigrants. One explanation, advanced by Pritchard: "Lifestyle is a powerful factor. [Immigrant Blacks] are three times less likely to smoke than American –born Blacks, according to NIH research, and far less likely to be obese. [Immigrant Blacks] drink less and exercise more, according to other federal research (Pritchard, 2004). Pritchard goes on with "As they assimilate, however, many immigrants adopt bad health habits. Research by Singh and others suggest that, over time, immigrants behave like the American-born population – more of them smoke, drink, and gain weight" (Pritchard, 2004).

Armas reports that "...difference between Black Immigrants and native-born Blacks have created friction in some communities." These tensions are most apparent in cities where Immigrant Blacks have settled in large numbers. In New York and South Florida "political tensions have risen when an election pits a native-born candidate against an Afro-Caribbean one" (Armas, 2004). Differences such as these, recently referred to as "thorny issues" on the Harvard University campus are manifest. Rimer and Arenson reported that while "about 8 percent , or about 530, of Harvard's undergraduates were Black, Lani Guinier, a Harvard law professor, and Henry Louis Gates, Jr., the chairman of Harvard's African and African-American studies department, point out that the majority of them – perhaps as many as two-thirds – were West Indian and African immigrants or their children, or to a lesser extent, children of biracial couples...only about a third of the students were from families in which all four grandparents were born in this country, descendents of slaves" (Rimer and Areson, 2004). "What concerned the two professors, according to Rimer and Arenson" was that in the high-stakes world of admissions to the most selective colleges – and with it, entry into the country's inner circles of power, wealth and influence – African-American students whose families have been in America for generations are being left behind" (Rimer and Areson, 2004).

This concern may be supported by data. Beveridge, "a sociologist at Queens College, says that among 18-25 –year-old Blacks nationwide, about 9 percent describe themselves as of African or West Indian ancestry." This datum juxtaposed with the finding of "Researchers at Princeton University and the University of Pennsylvania who have been studying …minority students at 28 …colleges and universities…that 41 percent of the Black students identified themselves as immigrants, as children of immigrants or as mixed race" tend to lend validity to the concern of Guinier, a Harvard law professor, and Henry Louis Gates (Rimer and Areson, 2004).

The under representation of American-born Blacks in these higher education populations may predict friction and tension on campuses. In practice, the behavior of some American-born Blacks has been impacted. They now refer to themselves as "the descendants" (Rimer and Areson, 2004).

Pritchard suggests future diminishing differences in conditions and outcomes for immigrant versus American-born Blacks, and Clayola Brown, civil rights director for the Union of Needletrades Industrial and Textile Employees suggests that (1) the Paradise enjoyed by Black immigrants may be in the process of being or may have already been lost and (2) American –born Blacks do not know, as might be predicted, that Black immigrants encounter the same racism and stereotypes encountered by native-born Blacks. "They are often perceived as lazy, criminals, drug dealers and welfare cheats. This perception often results in police harassment, intimidation, unlawful arrests and even murder" (Takougang (Undated).

"Many American [-born] Blacks," according to Brown, "do not realize those born oversees must overcome the same disparities in housing, education and health care [as] they do…" (Armas, 2004). Butcher (1990), for example, observes that "Although immigrant Blacks, by some criteria, outperform native Blacks, there are still large disparities between their success and that of native whites."

Taken together, it may be the case that immigrant Blacks are now enjoying a kind of halo effect. Will the halo endure? If not, what is in store for immigrant Blacks at the point in time at which they become "one of us?" This question has, to some extent, been discussed in Chapters Two, Three, and four of *Cultural and Educational Excellence Revisited*. Perhaps, however, an equally salient question will be whether or not immigrant and native-born Blacks become one because of actions taken by external power and authority or by our own authority and design.

Earlier reference was made to tension between Black Immigrants and native-born Blacks in cities and communities where Immigrant Blacks have settled in large numbers. African immigrants, often in response to such tension have begun to organize in "order to become a more powerful political and economic force in their respective communities" (Takougang, Undated). A partial list of such groups provided by (Takougang, Undated) includes the "All African Peoples Organization in Omaha, Nebraska, the Nigerian-American Chamber of Commerce in Miami, The Tristate (Ohio, Indiana and Kentucky) Cameroon Family, the Nigerian Women Eagles Club in Cincinnati, Ohio, and the African Heritage Inc. in Wisconsin.

It is for these and other reasons that I find it incumbent upon those of us who exert control over social and educational systems and subsystems to cast a wider net and commit to saving all learners of African descent. Perhaps this commitment to and expectation for all learners of African descent was best expressed in the NABSE report titled *Saving the African American Child*:

> We expect the school to expand the scope of knowledge and to develop the rational reflective and critical capacities of our children. We have every right to expect that, upon completion of public school work, our children will have the general skills to enter the world of work and to be fully functional members of the society. But more than this, we want the content of education to be *true, appropriate, and relevant*. We want the educational processes to be *democratic* and *humane*. We want the *aim* of education to be the complete development of the person, and not merely preparation for the available low-level jobs, or even for high-level jobs, that may serve no purpose beyond individual enhancement."

The reality is that all Americans of African descent find themselves, in Dunbar's terms, "gathahed hyeah,...In dis howlin' wildaness." It is also the case that we have a responsibility to save our collective progeny without regard to the conditions in which we find that we must toil for "individual enhancement." As we attend to this responsibility we would be wise to observe Ron Edmonds' three three declarative statements:

(1) We can, whenever and wherever we choose, successfully teach all children whose schooling is of interest to us;

(2) We already know more that we need to do that; and

(3) Whether or not we do it must finally depend on how we feel about the fact that we haven't so far"

A controlling question then becomes one of: Is it in our collective interest to save all children of African descent? An affirmative answer suggests the need to recommit to *Knowing, Doing, Being and Becoming as though Saving the African American Child Matters* – a commitment that is "...*true, appropriate,....relevant...democratic* and *humane;* that accommodates the proclivities of learners of African descent as they have been shaped and honed by experience, and that renders us able to *know, do, be and become* as did the Centurion who commanded that "they which could swim should cast themselves first into the sea and get to land. And the rest, some on boards and some on broken pieces of the ship. And so it came to pass, that they escaped all safe to land.

JAJR

JULY 2004

HOUSTON, TEXAS

In reflection of both the 1984 *Saving the African American Child* report and what the authors of *Knowing, Doing, Being and Becoming as though Saving the African American Child Matters*, my attention focuses on cultural biases and school climate factors influenced by standardized testing which, in turn, leads to the potential of placing the African American student in special services. As reported in the 1984 report, "standardized tests in America have more often been instruments of politics than instruments of science (psychology or education). Where African American children are concerned the results have been disastrous (NABSE, 1984, p.27). Standardized testing is the basis for ability grouping for classroom environments from gifted and talented to remedial learners to the referral and placement of students in special education. The African American student too often falls into the special education component due to the lack of learning opportunities, be it home or school to be successful on these tools used to measure achievement.

"The phenomenon of culturally linguistically diverse (National Research Council (CLD)) learners and special education, disproportionalism is not a recent concern" (National Research Council, 2002). The labeling and placement of African American students dates back to initial drives to integrate the public school system. The placing of an African American student with a teacher unaware of culture, learning style training, behavior and teaching strategies to help assist in the teaching the African American learner, developed the foundation of today in the ever growing population of African Americans in special education. Standardized test used to place the African American student in special education are suspect to the character injustices as the only key factor placing the student in special services.

Cultural biases may be associated with low teacher expectations and constant negative feedback. As reflected on student learning, reported in Chapter IV of *Cultural and Educational Excellence Revisited*, is not only experienced by the African American learners sitting in the classroom with a white teacher, it is experienced by African American learners with a teacher of their same ethnicity as well. Teachers often fail to provide the necessary encouragement and enrichment to minority and poor students because their expectations of those students' success are low (Educational Testing Service 1991). Cultural biases affect the curriculum as well. Curriculum for low academic achievers is one of stale comparison to that of the student in college preparatory classes. If one teaches poorly then one can only expect the students to perform minimally, if at all. Cultural biases cause anxiety and an inferiority complex. America's emphasis on innate ability is likely to have especially negative consequences for African Americans anxiety about racial stereotypes and intellectual competence can even depress their performance on standardized test (Jencks, Phillip 1998). According to Geneva Gay, "Multiculturalism should be the driving force of subsequent efforts to desegregate school curricula. It is a reconstructive and transformative principle. Its application necessitates changing the fundamental value assumptions, substantive content, operational strategies, and evaluation procedures of all instructional programs that are planned and implemented for all students "(Gay, 1990, p. 72).

In the 2002, the National Alliance of Black School Educators' report to school administrators, *Addressing the Over-Representation of African American Students in Special Education,* the authors' cited school climate as a contributing factor. School climate can markedly affect over representation. Administrators, faculty, and staff bring into the workplace their own assumptions, theories and beliefs about students. Branding and possible over identification of African American students, placing them in special education is due, in part, to a lack of cultural diversity training on the part of the educators in the classroom. How can educators reduce the possible desire to place the African American student in special education? A positive school climate is imperative in developing the young minds of the African American student. The 2002 National Alliance of Black School Educators' report expounds on this topic by suggesting to administrators that; Beyond understanding the role of climate in encouraging the capabilities and emphasizing the worth of individuals, the educational needs of African American students must be respected. A school climate that respects individual differences and embraces diversity may contribute to the decline of students being referred to special education, thus reducing the numbers of African American students disproportionately represented in special education. It is important that African American students have teachers free of bias, who concentrate on the teaching and instructing of learners based on their abilities, and developing learners' strengths as well as weaknesses.

It is believed that to improve the academic achievement of students in the public school system, a national testing system should emerge. The ideology still will not deter the problem of instructional delivery and motivation lacking in the classrooms of the average African American student, but could provide a source for an even playing field as well as national scope of the problem. Outcomes for students in relation to the curriculum should be conducted in numerous ways, not just one, which may or may not determine the students' academic path through school. In special education numerous methods are used to assess the student's achievement during the school year. Why can these methods not be utilized for assessing the academic achievement of all students? Performance-based instruction, portfolios as well as ongoing assessment should be utilized to assess student performance in the classroom. The National Coalition of Advocates for Students, advocates for equity in educational excellence, and insists that the role of student assessment can be a constructive one only if it is defined within the context of an education restructuring process that includes standards for equity in educational resources and processes that determine students' "real life" opportunities to learn (NCAS, Tate 1993).

Tests used to place students in special services are biased in the fact that it is culturally based on and developed by middle class Caucasian males who assume all Reflections on *Cultural and Educational Excellence Revisited* students tested, have been provided with the same equal opportunities of exposure to culture, experiences and learning practices. Standardized testing should ensure cultural competence as well as assess the level of academic achievement. Both play a vital role in assessing the true levels of competence of the African American student. Standardized testing should not be a saving grace for removing the unexposed, unruly students from the ill prepared teacher's classroom. Administrators, teachers, and staff should evoke cultural competence within the classroom. Cultural competence assumes that individuals are able to relate and communicate effectively with individuals who do not share the same culture, ethnicity and/or language (NABSE, 2002).

According to the U. S. Department of Education, for the school year 1998-1999 Black students accounted for 14.8% of the student population accounted for 20.2% of the students in programs for students with disabilities. The discrepancies for Black students fall primarily in the high incidence categories, including mild mental retardation or serious emotional disturbance (Cartedge, 2003). Eighty-four percent of all Blacks in special education are male (Grant, 1992). With such a high number of males in special education, there is obviously a disconnect in the teaching and reaching out to the African American male population. But could it actually be the limited exposure to what is asked of them on intelligence/achievement batteries?

In the 1984 National Alliance of Black School Educators Report, their argument was and to this day prevails, "How can placement occur through alienated cultured content?" The standardized test makers of the Wood-cock- Johnson Psycho-Educational Battery and the Wechsler Intelligence Scale for Children, common instruments used to test and place African American students, were just recently revised within the past three years to become more" minority friendly" as well as updating to the current trends in today's society. Gone from the test are the cup and saucer and rotary phone identification common items missed by African American students referred for special services, due to lack of exposure.

Differentiated instruction and behavioral support ought not be something that a student receives in special education, but rather something that is basically the right of every student in public education. To address the disproportionate placement, we must address these variables in the regular education classroom and preclude the failure that otherwise would lead to assessment and eventually special education placement. Before looking for what is "wrong" with the student, we must look to see what may be lacking in the environment that contributes to their failure.

KAL

2005

HOUSTON, TEXAS

As we look at the condition of culture and education for Americans of African decent, introductory comments from *Saving The African American Child* are enlightening. It is stated, in the beginning of this report that "...*quality* and *excellence* in education for African Americans includes: excellence in the 'basic skills,' in liberal, vocational, economic, political, and spiritual education. But it includes, in addition, excellence in ridding our people of all vestiges of miseducation. This means that we must know ourselves and our condition" (NABSE 1984, p. 14). These comments still hold true today and set the stage for our work in *Cultural And Educational Excellence Revisited: Knowing, Doing, Becoming and Being as though Saving the African American Child Matters,* and for my reflections.

Our history and our experiences clearly lead me to conclude that if we are to better ourselves, we must know ourselves and we must understand ourselves. As we look back at the years of inequalities and the thoughts and words of our ancestors who often addressed the impact of the "miseducation" of the African American, it becomes even clearer that if we are to *know how to do, know what to do and how to become what we need to be to achieve academic excellence for our children* now and in the future then we must contribute to that better understanding. There are several questions that consistently plague my thoughts and continue to influence my research. First, how dependent is our quality of education on the quality of life in our community? Second, is the educational future of our children predetermined by the conditions from which we come? My reflections are directed towards these two questions.

Chapter 2 of *Cultural And Educational Excellence Revisited: Knowing, Doing Becoming and Being as though Saving the African American Child Matters* addresses the cultural performances of Americans of African descent. The research in this chapter has posed the question, "How do the cultural performances of Americans of African descent compare with the cultural performances of Americans of non-African descent? The authors, Cummings, Johnson and Bailey-Perry, examined nine social progress indicators: education, elected politicians, employment, health, homeownership, incarceration, income, longevity and wealth. The findings of the authors led to the conclusion that the cultural performances of Americans of African descent may not be judged as excellent. This conclusion may be drawn, in part, due to several phenomena that are briefly summarized in the following paragraph.

First, our research found significant gaps in performance in education. Specifically, there were gaps in college enrollment, in college completion rates and a persistent gap in performance on standardized tests. Second, we have been and continue to be under-represented in politics. Several decades after the civil rights movement the number of elected African American politicians is shrinking. Third, an examination of the labor market revealed that unemployment rates for African Americans have consistently doubled that of whites. African Americans on average earn less than white Americans with the same qualifications. Fourth, and even more alarming have been our statistics on health and longevity. These statistics reflected higher percentages of over-weight individuals, prevalence of diabetes, higher death rates from heart disease and stroke, higher infant mortality rates, higher prostate cancer rates and increased incidences of death from AIDS. African Americans have the highest death rate of any of America's racial and ethnic groups. Fifth, the statistics on home ownership have indicated that African Americans are less likely to own their own homes than their white counterparts. Lastly, the criminal justice system has had a disproportionate impact on African American males. It is evident from this discussion of social progress indicators that the cultural performances of Americans of African descent may not be judged as excellent, according to the NABSE definition of excellent cultural performance, "when the group's birth rate exceeds its death rate, infant mortality is below normal, the mortality rate of the group is superior to the average and the progeny are more successful than the parent group in social progress…" (NABSE, 1984, p. 23).

Clearly, an understanding of these cultural performances is significant to an understanding of ourselves and will lead us to the development of strategies and solutions that will support improving academic performance. Even though the preponderance of evidence positions us to conclude that our cultural performance may not be excellent, the rich history of struggle that has been waged over many years to secure the benefits of citizenship, access to public and private education and equal protection of the law, we must be emboldened by the fact that we have not lost our courage nor have we ever fallen victim to defeat.

How dependent, then, is our quality of education on the quality of life in our community? Is our educational future already predicted by the conditions from which we come? There is no question that our schools are confronted with constraints that are influenced by the environment from which our children come. But, our expectation has been, and will always be, that our children who enter the educational system, will be transformed into educated individuals who will enjoy a quality of life superior to that enjoyed by their parents.

Clearly, the state of our condition rests on many factors as we have indicated in our earlier discussion of social progress indicators. Many critics will argue that the improvement of our condition rests heavily on our cultural performance, but it is my belief that our cultural performance does not and should not foretell or predict our academic outcome. The achievement of academic excellence, rests in our hands and will be a continuing struggle for African Americans. We must be up to the challenge and continue to evaluate our condition, seeking resources and developing programs that will address the state of our condition.

The Center for the Development and Study of Effective Pedagogy for African American Learners (CPAL) at Texas Southern University is an example of a successful response to this challenge. Founded by Dr. Jay Cummings and a group of educators in 1994, this educational think-tank addressed the needs of African American children from Low-income families and provided much needed support for these students. An analysis of (Texas) state reports of student performance (PEIMS and AEIS reports) determined that there was a discrepancy between the performance of economically disadvantaged students and those who were not. There was clearly a need to provide academic assistance that would supplement what was currently being provided in order to close the existing achievement gap.

It was the mission of CPAL to promote educator and institutional responsibility for the excellent and equitable education of African American learners. In its efforts to promote educator and institutional responsibility, CPAL focused teaching, research and service on improving the capacities of educators and educational institutions to work effectively with African American students. The CPAL mission was based on Ron Edmond's philosophy *"The educability of students derives far more from the nature of the school to which they are sent than it derives from the nature of the family from which they come."*

CPAL accomplished its mission through a series of initiatives relative to teaching, professional development, support and service to teachers, school officials and school-community stakeholders. Furthermore, these initiatives were specific to the improvement of the capacities of educators and educational institution officials to assure the school success of African American and low-income learners on state, mandated assessments.

Under the leadership of Dr. Sumpter Brooks and Dr. Danita Bailey-Perry, each year following its inception, CPAL accomplished its mission by partnering with community schools and providing opportunities for parents, teachers, school officials and community stakeholders to participate in training and services relative to improving students' academic performance in a variety of content areas, especially in the areas of Reading and Mathematics.

CPAL sponsored activities included the convening of the CPAL National Advisory Board, the documentation of success stories and success strategies of schools that worked successfully with African American students, research, an annual summer institute during which stakeholders (parents, students, teachers, administrators, community leaders, business partners, university faculty and state administrators) participated in brainstorming and instructional activities and site specific professional development activities that were provided to individual schools.

In each CPAL sponsored activity program staff worked towards the following goals:

- To identify and provide professional development and site specific services and needs to CPAL partnership schools.
- To determine the instructional needs and support services for CPAL partnership school communities to accomplish their instructional goals.
- To assist institutional officials and individual educators in changing attitudes and practices that are barriers to education excellence and equity with respect to reading, writing, mathematics, science, ssocial studies, cultural and other subjects and other subjects relative to the Texas Assessment system (TAKS, TEKS, TAAS, and TASP).
- To research, study, design and implement culturally consistent educational pedagogy.

The CPAL mission, and that of similar groups, is paramount to the successful performance of African American children. The challenges we face require continued support for parents, teachers and schools who serve African American and lower-income students. These challenges also require the continuous monitoring and evaluation of our condition, the unrelenting researching and studying of effective pedagogy and instructional strategies, the development of models and the identification of best practices. The CPAL project should be viewed as an example of how we can rally resources to develop and support the needs of our students. We must continue to create, to implement, to examine and to evaluate the efficacy of such models as we have much *to learn, to do, be, and become* as we continue the struggle towards academic excellence. Our mission, should we choose to accept it, is to take on the challenge of offering an education to our children that is academically and culturally excellent, even when the odds are against us.

MDBP

2005

HOUSTON, TEXAS

CHAPTER SIX

UNFINISHED BUSINESS

As we revisited *Cultural And Educational Excellence,* areas of need for more and better knowledge and practice became apparent. In this chapter we share a set of needs that we deem most critical for the information and action of stakeholders who have an interest in and commitment to saving the African American child. We do so with the belief that researchers, practitioners, parents, community business, religious, and opinion leaders who have an interest in and commitment to saving the African American child in concert with funding sources may consider our list — the extent to which these needs are reduced, will be the extent to which we may approach educational and cultural excellence with profit and interest.

- School performance of learners of African descent must be compared with school performances of white and Asian American students.

- Identified gaps in school performance must be analyzed and explained - taking into consideration such probable causes as (a) teaching children and youth of African descent a curriculum that is different from the curriculum taught to other students (tracking), (b) exposing African American learners to lower-level and less rigorous curricula; (c) assigning teachers who have not demonstrated effective teacher behavior as measured by results with learners of African descent to teach African American children and youth, (d) expecting less of African American learners (lower standards) and (e) creating inappropriately large classes.

- Fundable initiatives must be developed, funded, implemented and monitored that address highly probable causes of identified gaps in school performance with African American versus Asian and white learners.

- "Prevention rather than treatment should be the driving force in dealing with diet, alcohol consumption, tobacco use and exercise…People need to understand that they don't need to take a fatalistic view, he goes on, lifestyle changes can have a tremendous impact; about 80 percent of cancers can be influenced by lifestyle"(Hoover, 1999).

- Assessment that focuses on "What was taught" as opposed to "What was learned" needs to be addressed. Assessment practices designed to compare school performance with "What was taught" often results in a failure to examine and measure what, in fact, was learned. While it is recognize that the current high-stakes-testing-accountability environment requires that schools and systems demonstrate compliance with national, state, and district standards; the need to know, independent of these standards, what the learner has, in fact, learned or achieved remains critical. To quote from *Saving the African American Child:*

  "While scientists have recommended that the priority purpose for standardized testing and assessment in the schools should be to improve the quality of student achievement. Tests have most often been used to confirm the fact that teaching has failed" (p.27-28).

- Assumptions of white supremacy in the context of schooling must be challenged when they influence what students learn, what teachers teach, how schools are managed, and how educational policy is formulated, approved, as well as implemented.

- Cultural performances should continue to be monitored and evaluated. Resulting information should be used to direct further research and to establish partnerships and organizational entities that will support improved social progress in each of the social progress indicators examined in this book.

- Preventive measures should be taken to mitigate against high incidence rates of cancer.

- Research and service must be focused on improving the ability of educators to work successfully with African American children.

- The curriculum to which learners of African descent are exposed should be examined. Systems expectations for these learners must reflect the belief that "a high level of academic achievement is within reach of virtually all African American children," (NABSE, p.35). This belief must be manifested in (1) ending the practice of "tracking" or sentencing learners of African descent to schooling characterized by mediocrity and post schooling meager qualities of life, (2) ending the practice of exposing learners of African descent to schooling characterized by low level basic skills and fundamental processes only and (3) exposing learners of African descent to the standards deemed to be vital by NABSE in its 1984 report titled *Saving the African American Child*.

- Effective educational leaders who produce increased academic achievement for students should think and act outside of traditional school operational and organizational parameters. They must pursue excellence, equity and legitimacy with purpose, passion, and commitment while analyzing the social context that empowers schools to protect the status quo with respect to power relationships.

- Models for practice based on successful schools, successful teaching and research results must be identified and developed.

- State legislators should comprehend the educational needs of diverse learners of African descent as well as diverse learners from low-income home environments.

- Resource allocation behavior of school leadership, i.e., assigning neophytes to teach learners from low income families of African descent, failing to allocate resources as a function of the educational needs of learners from low income families of African descent (that is disproportionate to our numbers in order to meet the educational and cultural excellence needs of African American children and youth), and providing Eurocentrically–biased textbooks should be addressed.

- The management of instruction in schools that serve learners of African descent is in need of examination. NABSE's *Saving the African American Child* report suggests criteria by which performances of school personnel who control school systems and subsystems may be assessed:
  - √ They support some organization that has the education of African American learners as its priority (p.34).
  - √ The *content* of education is *true, appropriate,* and *relevant* (p.15).
  - √ The educational *processes* are *democratic* and *humane* (p.15).
  - √ Intervention components to foster improvements in the character of the content of education are in place (p.25).
  - √ Learners of African descent are prepared for self-knowledge and to become contributing problem-solving members of their communities and in the wider world as well (p.15).
  - √ "It is not enough to set equal test 'standards of excellence' for admission to and exit from schools. The equitable quality of educational treatment itself must be guaranteed. Equal exit standards for students without equitable school treatment of them are grossly unfair" (p.22).
  - √ The school offers an education that is excellent academically and culturally (p.29).
  - √ There is independent, systematic, ongoing community–initiated and community-sponsored out-of-school educational activities for African American learners (p.30).

√ *"Excellence in teaching is reflected first and foremost is the achievement of the students of the teachers"* (p.33).

√ African American learners have an equal opportunity to master new technologies (p.34).

√ *Discipline* is construed as "the student's ability and the will to do what need doing for as long as it need doing and to learn from the results" (p.37).

• The academic achievement growth, if any, of the African American student in special education should be reviewed.

• The behavior and/or academic attitudes of the African American male student in special education in relation to athletics should be reviewed.

• Funding for the development of programs that seek to improve the academic performance of African American children should be sought.

• The effectiveness of the new WISC and WJ-III and the placement of African American students in referral for potential placement into Special Education should be studied.

• The backgrounds of special educators in relation to curricula they are assigned to teach as well as extents to which they are successful with special education students should be studied.

• Teaching methods to which learners of African descent are exposed should be examined. For example, Eurocentric linear approaches are often incongruent with the natures and needs of learners who come to school having mastered curvilinear learning skills and abilities. It is often the case that school expectations are incompatible with the background and experience of learners of African descent as well. Relatedly, Saving the African American Child states "We do reject categorically the model that places the reasons for failure in our children rather than in the systems which fail them…Do we need special re-mediation for those who were never "mediated?" NO!! (p. 29).

- African Americans should be encouraged to "…get the advanced medical care that can mean the difference between life and death" (Hoover, 1999).

- Training and professional development to which school administrators and teachers are exposed need to be aligned with areas in which school performances with learners of African descent are in need of improvement.

- Educational achievement gaps are subject to documentation and deserve immediate attention. Questionable educational practices that label and brand students for success or failure permeate the delivery of instruction to students from culturally, socially, economically, and linguistically diverse families and home environments. Educators should understand students within the context of their home and school environments. This will help one's actions towards that student to be more appropriate, rather than grouping students based on a particular characteristic (*stereotyping*).

- Thinking outside of the box may provide an avenue to reach someone who had previously been deemed unreachable. The utilization of innovative alternatives in lieu of what some may categorize as traditional methods, may be beneficial. This will provide each student an opportunity to learn.

- Educators should be resourceful and willing and able to recognize certain indicators that may require one to refer a student to other services within the school setting, such as counseling. This will foster student growth.

- Educators should focus on each student's capabilities. Often times student's are recognized and separated based on limitations. However, what is the student capable of? Once his/her capabilities are recognized and understood, build on them. This will help self-esteem.

CHAPTER SEVEN

INFORMATION ABOUT THE AUTHORS

Dr. Shanna L. Broussard has an undergraduate degree from Southern University at Baton Rouge; an M.S. and Rh.D. from Southern Illinois University at Carbondale. Prior to pursuing her educational endeavors, she joined the United States Army as a Telecommunication Circuit Controller. During her service in the military, her tour of duty relocated her to Camp Casey Korea for a one year tour. Once she was released from active duty with an honorable discharge, she began her educational journey.

While she was in school in Illinois between 1997 and 2000, she held various positions that include Program Director for the Drug Elimination Program with the Jackson County Housing Authority; and Residential Counselor at Southern Illinois University at Carbondale's Evaluation and Development Center. Following her graduation, Dr. Broussard entered the academia arena. She has been afforded the opportunity to work at Southern University at Baton Rouge, Louisiana; Langston University in Oklahoma City, Oklahoma; and Texas Southern University in Houston, Texas. Dr. Broussard accepted a position at Texas Southern University in 2002 and has taught several classes on the master's and doctorate level within the Department of Counseling. The courses taught include Human Growth and Development, Theories of Counseling, Professional Orientation to Agency Counseling, Counseling and Personality Theories, Introduction to Career Development in Counseling, Individual Appraisal in Counseling, and Individual and Case Management in Counseling.

She currently holds several memberships with various professional organizations such as Texas Counseling Association, and the National Association for African American Studies. Additionally, in 2003, she was named an Emerging Leader with TCA. Dr. Broussard has deep interests that revolve around diversity and community awareness. Feel free to contact Dr. Broussard at broussard_sl@tsu.edu.

Dr. Jay R. Cummings holds a baccalaureate degree from Central State University, an M.Ed. from Cleveland State University and a Ph.D. from The Ohio State University. He has served in various roles with numerous public educational entities. These include, but are not limited to: teacher and administrator in the Cleveland, Ohio Public Schools; Graduate Research Associate and Assistant Director, Black Education Center at Ohio State University; Research Coordinator, Louisiana Board of Elementary and Secondary Schools; various roles (including Director, Personnel Development/Management Academy, Gifted Education, Director, State and Federal Programs and Staff Associate to The Study of Instruction) in the Dallas Independent School District; Adjunct Professor in Master of Human Services Program at Saint Edward's University; various senior management roles (including Assistant Commissioner for Federal Funds; Deputy Commissioner for Special Programs; Executive Deputy Commissioner for Programs and Instruction and State Director for Vocational Technical Education; and Special Assistant to the Commissioner of Education for Federal Policy Implementation at the Texas Education Agency); Associate Professor, Educational Administration Program at the University of North Texas and Dean of the College of Education at Texas Southern University in Houston, Texas.

While working at an inner city junior high school in a large midwestern city, Dr. Cummings was selected for a Ford Fellowship at the Ohio State University in Columbus, Ohio. Upon completion of the program of study in 1974, he was selected by the late Dr. Francis S. Chase, Dean Emeritus, University of Chicago to join a team of Fellows to study the instructional programs of the Dallas, Texas Independent School District. At the conclusion of that study, Dr. Cummings served as the Research Director for Louisiana Master Plan Project at the Louisiana State Board of Elementary and Secondary Education. In 1993, he was appointed an Academic Specialist for Tertiary Institutions in the Republic of South Africa.

Dr. Cummings served as the president of the National Association of State Directors of Vocational and Technical Education consortium; technical advisor to the Evaluation of Regional Educational laboratories; and founder for the Center for the Development and Study of Effective Pedagogy for African American Learners (CPAL) at Texas Southern University and the Texas and Dallas Alliances of Black School Educators (TABSE). He served Dallas Alliances of School Educators (TABSE). He served as President, TABSE; Chair, Vocational Technical Institutions for the Southern Association of Colleges and Schools; member of editorial board NABSE Journal; Executive Council, Commission on Middle and High Schools (SACS); Chair, CPAL Advisory Committee; and member, of the Independent Advisory Panel Advisory Committee; and member of the Independent Advisory Panel for the National Assessment of Vocational Education (NAVE). He has been a consultant to numerous international, national, state and local governmental, social, economic, and educational institutions. He has lectured, led seminars, or taught courses at The Ohio State University, Texas Southern University, University of Houston, Southern University, Texas A&M – Commerce, Texas Woman's University, and St. Edward's University. In addition to authoring numerous technical reports, articles, and critiques on school reform issues, he managed, wrote, and published the National Alliance of School Educators' 1999 and 2000 manuscripts entitled *The Demonstration Schools/Communities Initiative*. Dr. Cummings served as a member of the editorial board for the NABSE Journal from 1998 to 2003. From 1998 to 2004, he has been a member of the Executive Council for the Commission on Secondary and Middle Schools for the Southern Association of Colleges and Schools (SACS) and the Independent Advisory Panel as well as Technical Review Panel for the National Assessment of Vocational Education (NAVE).

As a Professor in the Department of Educational Administration and Foundations at Texas Southern University and Associate Professor at the University of North Texas in Denton, he has taught Politics in Education,

Instructional Leadership, Principles of Educational Administration, School and Community Relations, School Law, Issues in Educational Administration, and Clinical Supervision.

Dr. James A. Johnson, Jr. has an undergraduate degree from the City University of New York, a MS from Nova University, and a Ph.D. from the University of California. While in New York City, he served in various roles with numerous private and public social and educational agencies. Appointed as a Ford Foundation Fellow in 1968, Dr. Johnson interned with the Washington Internships in Education, serving as Special Assistant to the National Director of Head Start. From 1969 to 1973, he served in various roles including Associate Director at the Far West Laboratory for the Educational Research and Develop in San Francisco. In January of 1974, he became Associate Superintendent for Planning, Research and Evaluation in the Public Schools of the District of Columbia serving until August of 1975 when he became Executive Director of the Louisville Education Consortium and an Associate Professor at the University of Louisville. He accepted a professorship in Public Administration and Early Childhood Education at Nova University in 1977 and later served as National Professor and Director of Instruction in Nova's National Doctoral Program for School Administrators until 1989.

In January 1990, Dr. Johnson was appointed Director of the Division of Special Programs Planning and Implementation of the Texas Education Agency (TEA). He later served as Coordinator of the Divisions of Instruction and Instructional Technical Assistance and as Planner in the Office of the Executive Deputy Commissioner of Education. While at the Texas Education Agency, he authored or served as Senior Editor of such reports as *Responsible Education: A Plan to Education All Children, Educational Equity Through Barrier Reduction*, and the 1995-97 and 1997-99 *Texas State Plan to Reduce the Dropout Rate*. He also served with Dr. Jay Cummings as co-architect of Texas Southern University's Center for the Development and Study of Effective Pedagogy for African American Learners (CPAL) and served as TEA's Program Manager of the CPAL Contracts/Grants.

Dr. Johnson served as Vice-President of the St. George's Senior Housing, Inc. Board of Directors and as a member of the Public Sector Industry Committee, Greater Austin @ Work Summit. He also served as an Associate member of Texas Southern University's Center for the Development and Study of Effective Pedagogy for African American Learners' (CPAL) Advisory Board. National Alliance of School Educator (NABSE) positions held include Chair, Program Development, Research and Evaluation Commission; Member, NABSE Executive Board; President and Founder, NABSE Council of Affiliate Presidents; Co-author, NABSE publication entitled *Saving the African American Child*; President, the Ft. Lauderdale, Florida and Austin, Texas NABSE Affiliates; and Board Member, Texas Alliance of School Educators. He is in his fifth year as a participating member of NABSE's Demonstration Schools Initiative [Task Force III.] The Task Force is charged with identifying K-12 schools that provide exemplary educational services to learners of African descent as indicated by criterion and norm reference test scores.

Dr. Johnson has been a consultant to numerous federal, state and local governmental, social and educational institutions. He has lectured, led seminars or taught courses on three University of California campuses; at the Universities of Louisville and Kentucky; the Claremont Graduate School; Merrit College; the University of Nebraska at Lincoln; and Howard, Nova, and St. Edward's Universities where he served as Associate Professor, Master of Arts in Human Services (MAHS). Courses taught included 6356, *Human Growth and Development through the Like Cycles; Management and Diversity; Funding Sources and Proposal Preparation;* and *Conflict Resolution: Topics and Settings.* Additionally, he served as Director of the MAHS Administrative Internship Program, Coordinator of the MAHS Conflict Resolution Program, faculty advisor to the MAHS Student Organization and on various St. Edward's University-wide, School of Education and MAHS committees. Dr. Johnson served as Dean of St. Edward's University's Master of Arts in Human Services program for four years. He has given leadership to his consulting firm, *Ediphicacion,* since 1997 as well.

In 2002 Dr. Johnson accepted the position of Associate Dean for Academic Affairs in the College of Education at Texas Southern University in Houston, Texas. He and his wife Shari, reside in Manvel, Texas.

Krista A. Levi is currently a Vocational Adjustment Coordinator at Nimitz High School, in the Aldine Independent School District. Ms. Levi has been in education for ten years. She has worked in Aldine for eight years and served her first two in the Deer Park Independent School District, all in the area of Special Education. Ms. Levi has worked the Special Education gamut: life -skills, inclusion facilitator, and resource teacher and served as an Educational Diagnostician for three years prior to her current position.

Ms. Levi is actively involved with the Association of Texas Professional Educators, and served the Aldine Local as Vice- President for 3 years. She is currently a campus representative for the organization. Ms. Levi has an undergraduate degree in Psychology with a History minor from Texas Southern University. A Master in Education with Special Education concentration and is currently a Doctoral student in Curriculum and Instruction at Texas Southern University. She received her teacher training through Region IV Alternative Certification Program Cycle 8. At the 2003 National Association of African American Studies, Ms. Levi presented the following abstract; *"A Comparison of Learning Disabled Students Academic Achievement in Biology."* A study on the effectiveness of the content mastery room/services in providing support for the learning disabled student on End of Course Exams.

Ms. Levi's philosophy of education is as follows; "I believe that children are our future, teach them well and let them lead the way, show them all the beauty they posses inside." Those are simple but yet powerful words from a Whitney Houston song, you hear played when it comes to educational commercials but these words should be an oath that anyone stepping into any classroom should make! These words root my philosophy of education that all children can learn! It is more than just a strategy, inventory or model, but about caring concern to teach today's children. Be it crack infested or gifted and talented the children need the to be educated to be successful productive citizens.

Teaching is about passion, the passion to touch lives that have yet to be touched! To give students experiences they may only read about in books, but can feel they have been there in some way. It is about working on their individualism and not teaching to the masses! It is about making sure or at least hoping that everything you share with your students will come back to them later in life and have them remember you as the person who taught them the skills

Education is about building bridges for students to the unknown as well as known world. It is about using curriculum in a meaningful way, not just to earn an exemplary status! I enjoy the challenges of teaching the slow learner! I want those student to know that they too can learn and they are special, not just "special ed." I want to continue to bring the beauty of our future, hope in learning in as well as out of the classroom!

Dr. Danita Bailey-Perry holds a baccalaureate degree from Fisk University, an M.A. degree from George Peabody College for Teachers (currently Vanderbilt-Peabody University) and a Ph.D. from The University Of Texas at Austin. She has served in various roles with numerous public and private entities. These include teacher in Dayton, Ohio and Houston, Texas, Department Chairperson in Spring Branch I.S.D., Director of Educational Services at Spring Shadows Glen and the West Oaks and HCA Houston Hospital Systems and Adjunct Professor at the University of Houston. She also served as the Academic Enhancement Administrator, Director Of University Scholars and an Associate Professor in the School Services at Prairie View A&M University; and Senior Coordinator Of Training and Professional Development at The Texas A&M University System for The Regents' Initiative of The Texas A&M University System, heading a noted faculty development initiative with all nine universities within this system. She is currently the Director of The Center For The Development and Study of Effective Pedagogy For African American Learners (CPAL) and an Assistant Professor in the Department Of Educational Administration and Foundations at Texas Southern University. She has received several grants for research and program development.

In March 1999, Dr. Bailey published her research study "Identifying Effective Classroom and Building Practices That Increase the Academic Performance of Students in Schools With Complex Student Populations."

The second phase of this research project was published in "Identifying School Conditions And Teacher Practices That Have Proven Effective In Increasing Mathematics And Reading Achievement For African-American Students In Schools With Substantial Minority Student Populations."

She also co-authored "Cultural Performances of Americans of African Descent: Using Indicators of Social Progress as Measures of Qualities of Life." Other research includes "At-Risk Parents: Developing Partnerships—Techniques And Strategies," and "The Proficiency Of The Masters In Education Certification Program's Practices And Instruction For Leadership And ExCET Examination Preparation."

Courses taught include School Public Relations, Instructional Leadership, Internship, Externship, Advanced Seminar In Educational Administration, Personnel Administration, Fundamentals Of Educational Administration, and Theory, Practice and Research.

Dr. Bailey-Perry heads her own consulting firm, Focus Development, where she is a successful consultant and motivational speaker, providing over 500 inspirational workshops on a variety of topics to parents, teachers, administrators, students and business professionals.

Dr. Bailey-Perry is a certified school administrator, supervisor and superintendent in the state of Texas. She is a frequent presenter to national organizations, a noted researcher, a successful grant writer and an active participant in community and university service.

She, along with her husband Cornelius and son, Barrett, reside in Houston, Texas.

CHAPTER EIGHT

REFERENCES CONSULTED

American Council on Education. (2002). <u>2001-2002: Nineteenth annual status report on minorities in higher education.</u> Washington, D.C.

AmeriStat Staff. (2002). "Homeownership Rates Divide Racial and Ethnic Groups." AmeriStat. Retrieved November 2002 from http://www.ameristat.org/Content/ NavigationMenu/Ameristat/Topics1/2000Census1/ Homeownership_Rates_Divide_Racial_and_Ethnic_Groups.htm

Ameristat Staff. (2002). "Race/Ethnicity." Ameristat. Retrieved November 2002 from http://www.prb.org/AmeristatTemplate.cfm?Section=RaceandEthnicity&Template=/ Topics.cfm&InterestCategoryID=244

Anonymous. (2004). "Many minority college students fail to graduate/Report says schools have done little to increase rates." Associated Press in the <u>Houston Chronicle.</u> 27 May 2004.

Anonymous. (Undated) "Resources." Retrieved April 2004 from http://www.arches.uga.edu/~dfbailey/resources.htm

Anonymous. (2003). Paper #2. Regarding Allison's *Bastard out of Carolina.* http://www.groshlife.com/mt/archives/000037.html

Anonymous. (2001). Improving Student Achievement: School Related Factors and Teacher Behavior that Contribute to Low Self –Image in Students. Northwest Regional Educational Laboratory.

Armas, Genaro C. (2004)."U. S. S, Immigrants see Cultural Gap." Associated Press in the <u>Houston Chronicle.</u> 09 May 2004.

Armas, Genaro, "Women, minorities still trail in pay race," <u>South Florida Sun-Sentinel,</u> March 21, 2003, p. 3 D.

Associated Press (10 November 2002). "Group looks to open doors for [B]lack coaches." Houston Chronicle. Pp. 2-3B

Associated Press (2002). "Texas students score lower on ACT exam." Houston Chronicle. P.28A.

Associated Press (2002). "Death rates decline for most categories." Houston Chronicle. P. 21A.

Barker, Joel Arthur. (Date unknown). The Business of Paradigms. Discovering the Future Series. Charhouse Learning Corporation. Minnesota.

Broussard, S. L., Johnson, J. A., Jr., and Levi, K. A. (2003). "The Educational Branding Hypothesis: Branding African American Learners at an Early Age." Unpublished paper, Houston, Texas: Texas Southern University.

Butcher, Kristen F. (1990). " Immigrants to the United States: A Comparison with Native s and Other immigrants." Princeton University. New Jersey.

Carter, Robert. (2002). "Culture and Students' Success." Educational Considerations. v.18 n.1 p.7-11, ERIC NO. EJ417703

Cartledge, Gwendolyn Ph. D.(2003). President's Commission on Excellence in Special Education Assessment and Indentification Task Force Minority Overidentification and Misidentification. Educational Testing Services

Cortez, Albert (2002). IDRA Newsletter. p 2.

Chideya, F. (1995). Don't Believe The Hype. New York:Penguin Books.

Cole. Marva. (2002) "How does the educational progress of the children and youth in each group compare with the educational progress of their parents?" Paper written for EDCI 944, Curriculum Theory. College of Education. Texas Southern University. Houston, Texas.

Coleman, Larry Delano Esq. (1985). "Brief of the Kansas City Citizens for Quality Education, Respecting Remedy, as Amicus Curiae." Retrieved April 2004 from http://www.duboislc.org/LarryColeman/LawBrief.html

Cummings, J., Wentz, P., and Frederick, P. (2002). "The Educated Person of the Future: Implications for Educational Leadership Training." Unpublished report.

Cummins, J. (1986). Empowering minority students: A framework of intervention. Howard Educational Review. Washington, D. C.

Defender News Service (2002). "Poverty rate rises, income declines." The Houston Defender. PP 1-4.

Edmonds, R. (1981), "The Characteristics of Effective Schools: Research and Implementation ." Paper presented to the National Conference on Education Issues, New York City. In National Alliance of School Educators. (1984). *Saving the African American Child.* Washington, D.C.

Ellison, Ralph. (March 1995). The Invisible Man. Second International Edition. Random House. New York.

Ellison, Ralph (1999). Juneteenth. Random House. New York.

Emery, Theo (2002). "Merit aid fails needy students, study says." Houston Chronicle. P. 19A.

Fackelmann, Kathleen. (2002, 26 November) "Mistrust of doctors widespread across the USA." USA Today. P. 9D.

Farber, Charles (1967). White Reflections on Power. William B. Eerdmans Publishing Company: Grand Rapids, Michigan.

Ferguson, Ronald. (December 2002). Addressing Racial Disparities in High-Achieving Suburban Schools. North Central Regional Educational Laboratory: Portland, Oregon

Flynn, Patrice, Ph.D (2002). "Employment Indicator: Statistics on Employment and Unemployment. Calvert Group Ltd. and Hazel Henderson. Retrieved November 2002 from http://www.calvert-henderson.com/employ2.pdf

Fordham, S. and Ogbu, John V. (1986). Students' school success: Coping with the burden of acting white. The Urban Review. Agathon Press, Inc., Vol. 18, No. 3.

Fullerton, Kevin, (2000). "Opening the Doors." The Austin Chronicle.

Gammon, Robert and Marcucci, Michele (2002 August 27). "Census: Racial income disparities abound." The Oakland Tribune. Retrieved November 2002 from http://www.oaklandtribune.com/cda/article/print/ 0,1674,82%257E1865%257E822355,00.html

Garfinkel, Irwin and Meyers, Marcia K. (1999). "Executive Summary: New York City Social Indicators 1997 - A Tale of Many Cities: Retrieved November 2002 from http://www.siscenter.org/1999execsummary.html

Gavin, James R.,III (1995). "Testimony to the Congressional Caucus Health Braintrust." Diabetes Forecast. Vol. 48. pp53(3).

Gay, Geneva. (September,1990). Achieving Educational Equity Through Curriculum Desegregation. Phi Delta Kappan (72) 1.

General Assembly of North Carolina. (2000, May). "Closing the Achievement Gap." House Bill 1547.

Gordon, Rebecca, Piano, Libero Della, Keleher, Terry. (1999). "Facing the Consequences: An Examination of Racial Discrimination in U. S. Public Schools." ERASE (Expose Racism and Advance School Excellence). Applied Research Center. Oakland, California.

Gottlieb, D. (1964). Teaching and learners: The views of Negro and White teachers. Sociology of Education, 37(4).

Grant, P. (1992). Using Special Education to destroy Boys. The Negro Educational Review, 63, 17-21.

Greider, William (1992). Who Will Tell the People, The Betrayal of American Democracy." Simon and Schuster. New York.

Harvey, L. (2003). *On Branding Humans*. From Southwest Nebraska Magazine. http://www.publicchristian.com/SNNColumns/branding.htm

Hatch, M.J. (2002). *Response to questions on branding*. University of Virginia.

http://www.instituteforbrandleadership.org/AskTheExperts.htm

Hellmich, Nanci, "Study: neighborhood stores have poor food choices," USA Today, August 5, 2003, 5D.

Hilliard, Asa. (2000). " Excellence In Education Versus High-Stakes Standardized Testing." Journal Of Teacher Education. Retrieved May 2004 from http://www.auburn.edu/~sidlema/1120/testingjournal.htm

Hilliard, Asa. (1988). "The Standards Movement: Quality Control or Decoy?" Condensed from a speech given at a Howard University Fall 1997 conference on "Moving Beyond Standards To Provide Excellence and Equity in the African-American Community." Rethinking Schools, Milwaukee.

Hilliard, Asa, Sizemore, Barbara, et al, (1984). *Saving the African American Child*. Washington, DC: National Alliance of School Educators.

Hirschman, Bill. (2000, December 24. Page 6B). "Minority grades rise on state exam." Sun- Sentinel. Fort Lauderdale, Florida.

Hoover, Felix (1999). "Columbus begins tracking early deaths by race."

Hoover, Eric (2001). "Average Score on the SAT and the ACT Hold Steady," The Chronicle Of Higher Education, A52.

Hout, Michael (2001). "Educational Progress For African Americans And Latinos In The United States From The 1950's To The 1990's: The Interaction Of Ancestry And Class." University Of California Berkley Survey Research Center.

Hoy, Wayne and Miskel, Cecil G. (1996). Educational Administration Theory, Research and Practice. McGraw-Hill, Inc. New York.

Hubli. (2002). "Grade and Explanations." The Hindi (2001). *Memorandum of Understanding between the Government of Andhra Pradesh (THE Karnataka Government) and the Government of Azim Premji Foundation.*

Isaac, Stephen and Michael, William (1981). Handbook in Research and Evaluation. Edits. San Diego.

Jackson, Derrick Z (2002). s sitting down for all wrong reasons now." Houston Chronicle. P. 21A.

Jackson, Derrick, Z. (2001, January 02. Page 17A). "College Athletes Graduation Gap Bowl." Sun- Sentinel. Fort Lauderdale, Florida.

Jencks, C. and Phillips, M. (1998). The –White Test Score Gap: Why it persists and What can be done. The Brookings Review (16) (2), 24-27.

Jerald, Craig. (2001). Dispelling the Myth Revisited: Preliminary Findings from a Nationwide Analysis of "High-Flying" Schools. Education Trust: Washington, D.C.

Jones, Lovell A. (2002). "Dismayed by disparities in quality of cancer care." Houston Chronicle. O8 July 20024.

Kennickell, Arthur B., "A Rolling Tide: Changes In The Distribution Of Wealth In The U.S., 1989-2001. http://www.faireconomy.org/econ/RWG/African-American_Debt.html

Kettner, P., Daley, J. and Nichols, A. Initiating Change In Organizations And Communities, 1985.

Klineberg, Steven L., "Houston's Economic and Demographic Transformations: Findings from the expanded 2002 Survey of Houston's Ethnic Communities. Rice University. Houston, Texas. 2002.

Kong, Deborah (2002). "Despite advances, parity still eludes Blacks, group says." Houston Chronicle. P 3A.

Knight Ridder Tribune News. (2003, February 9,) "Reforms to help those struggling on SATs." Houston Chronical. P. 5 B.

Lee Cynthia. (2002, November 21.) "Diabetes ad blitz targets Hispanics , at-risk minorities." Houston Chronicle. P. 12 A.

Lee, Debra L., (2002). "Program to help s build wealth." Houston Chronicle. P. 9C.

Mathews, Jay. (1999, December). "Arlington Cuts Lag in Minority Test Scores." The Washington Post On Line.

Mauer, Marc. The Crisis Of The Young African American Male And The Criminal Justice System. Prepared for the U.S. Commission on Civil Rights. April 15-19, 1999. http://www.tgsm.org/pdfdocs

McCarthy, M. S. (2002). Response to questions on branding. Miami University. http://www.instituteforbrandleadership.org/AskTheExperts.htm

McRobbie, Joan. (1998, December). "The Achievement Gap in California: Implications for a Statewide Accountability System." California School Boards Association 's Annual Conference in San Diego.

Memorandum to members of the district's school board from the superintendent of schools dated 17 August 2000 the subject of which was "Results of the ACT 2000 Assessment."

Montecel, Maria (2002). IDRA Newsletter. pp. 3-7.

National Alliance of Black School Educators (2002). "Addressing Over-Representation of African American Students in Special Education." A report of the National Alliance of School Educators, Inc. Washington, D.C.

National Alliance of Black school Educators. (1987). "Blueprint for Leadership: The Mission and The Model." A report of the National Alliance of School Educators, Inc. Task Force on the Educational Development Plan. Washington, D. C.

National Alliance of Black School Educators (2002). "Saving the African American Child." A report of the National Alliance of School Educators, Inc. Washington, D. C.

National Assessment of Educational Progress. (2000). "Performance of Students in Grades 4, 8, and 12." The Conditions of Education. Wysiwyg:24/http://nces.ed.gov/pubs2000/coe2000/section2/indicator14.html.

National Research Council. (2002). Minority Students in Special and Gifted Education. Washington, D.C.: National Academy Press.

Nel, Johanna (1992). The empowerment of minority students: Implications of Cummins' model for teacher education. Action in Teacher Education. 14(3).

Nissimov, Ron (2002). "Hispanics quit college at high rate." Houston Chronicle. pp. 27 and 29.

Olson, Lynn. (1996, December). "Achievement Gap Widening, Study Reports". Education Week On Line.

Patterson, Frederick D (1997). The African American Education Data Book, Vol. 1. Frederick D. Patterson Research Institute.

Patterson, Frederick D. (1997). "The African American Education Data Book. Volume II: Preschool through High School Education." Frederick D. Patterson Research Institute of the College Fund/UNCF. Fairfax, Virginia.

Pinderhughes, Elaine. Afro-American Families And The Victim System, In Ethnicity And Family Therapy, 1982.

Pritchard, Justin. (2004). "Immigrants outliving native-born Americans/Lifestyle, diet cited in 3-year difference." Associated Press in the Houston Chronicle. 27 May 2004.

Reugger, Maria and Robert Johns. Using Theories In Social Work, Using Systems Theory In Social Work Unit Workbook, 1996, p.28.

Rimer, Sara and Arenson, Karen W. (2004). "Top Colleges Take More s, but Which ones?" nytimes.com. June 24, 2004. http://query.nytimes.com/gst/abstract.html?res=F00917FC355D0C778EDDAF0894DC404482

Rodriquez, Erik (2002). More minorities enrolling in college." Austin American Statesman. Pp. 1-A-8.

Rodriquez, Lori. (2004). "Report: HPD frisks s 3 ½ times moe than whites/rRate for Latinos exceeds twice tht of Anglos. Houston Chronicle. O4 February 2004.

Ruegger, Maria and Johns, Robert. "Using Systems Theory In Social Work." (1996). The Open Learning Foundations, pp. 28-29.

Sable, Jennifer. (1998). "The Educational Progress of Students." http://nces.ed.gov/pubs98/condition98/c98003.html.

Salant (2002). "Nation's penal system encompasses 6.6 million." Houston Chronicle. Pp. 1 and 14A.

Schmoker, Mike. (2004). "Tipping Point: From Feckless Reform to Substantive Instructional Improvement: in Phi Delta Kappan. Volume 85, Number 6, Bloomington, Indiana: PDK International.

School Curriculum Bulletin, 2000-2001

Scripps Howard News Service (2002). "Alzheimer's called an 'epidemic' for Blacks." The Dallas Morning News.

Skertic,Mark, Guerrero, Lucio and Herguth, Robert (2002). "Same neighborhood, different worlds ." Chicago Sun-Times. Retrieved November 2002 from http://www.chicagosuntimes.com/output/census/cst-nws-census27.html

Simmons, Patrick (2000). "Shelter Indicators." Quality of Life Indicators. Calvert Group Ltd. and Hazel Henderson. Retrieved November 2002 from http://www.calvert-henderson.com/shelter1.pdf.

Snyder Mike (2002). "U. S. poverty rate rises." Houston Chronicle. P. 29.

Spera, Vincent. (1997, March). "Can Current Education Reform Efforts Close the Growing Achievement Gap?" Based on remarks made at an American Youth Policy forum held on March 14, 1987, on Capitol Hill.

Squyres, Pam (2000). "Losing Ground." Mother Jones Journal.

Task Force on Academic and Cultural Excellence. (1984). Saving the African American Child. Washington, D.C.: National Alliance of School Educators.

Task Force III. (2003). "Demonstration Schools/Communities Initiative Newsletter." Volume 01, Number 01, Washington, D.C.: National Alliance of School Educators.

Task Force III. (2001). "Site Visit Checklist: School/Community Eligibility Criteria." Unpublished document, Washington, D.C.: National Alliance of Black School Educators.

Texas Education Agency. Pocket Edition 1996-97 and 1997-98

Texas Education Agency. Selected State Academic Excellence Indicator System Data. Seven Year History. 1994-2000.

Texas Education Agency. 1999-2000 State Performance Report. State Academic Excellence Indicator System.

Takougang, Kjoseph. (2004) 'Contemporary African Immigarants to the United States. Taken down on 28 June 2004. http://www.afaricamigration.com/articles/jtakougang.htm

Thomas, Kiah. (2004). "Mr. Cosby, my name is 'Kiah.'" San Francisco Bay View. http://www.sfbayview.com/070704/mrcosby070704.shtml

Tirozzi, Gerald. (June 2004). "ESEA – What Happened to the 'S'." Retrieved June 2004 from http://www.principal.org/advocacy/views/esea_.cfm

University Of Pennsylvania - African Studies Center. (1993). "African-American Bibliography- Education." Retrieved April 2004 from http://www.sas. upenn.edu/African_Studies/Bibliography/AFAM_Education.html

The University of the State of New York. (1993). "An African-American Bibliography: Education." Retrieved May 2004 from http://www.historicaltextarchive.com/ sections.php?op=viewarticle&artid=45.

The United States Commission on Civil Rights (1999). "Volume I, The role of government and private health care programs and initiatives, the health care challenge: acknowledging disparity, confronting discrimination, and ensuring equality. Retrieved November 2002 from http://academic.udayton.edu/health/08civilrights/01-02-10Profile-AA.htm.

U.S. Census Bureau. (2000). Percent of people 25 years old and over who have completed high school or college, by race, Hispanic origin years 1940 to 2000. Washington, D.C.

Villafranca, Armando (2002, November 19). "A & M's diversity gains few." The Houston Chronicle. Pp 19 and 26 A.

Wessel, David. "Studies Suggest Potent Race Bias In Hiring," The Wall Street Journal. September 4, 2003.

Williams, David R. and Chiquita Collins, "Racial Residential Segregation: A Fundamental Cause Of Racial Disparities In Health," Public Health Reports. September-October 2001, Volume 116, pp. 404-416.

Wimberly, George. (2002). "School Relationships Foster Success for African-American Students." Retrieved June 2004 from http://www.ecs.org/html

Wissner, Sheila, "Locked Out Of The American Dream, Tennessean. May 4, 2003. http://cgi.tennessean.com/cgi-bn/print/pr.pl

Zuniga, Jo Ann and Janette Rodrigues, "Schools Boosting Technical Skills But Reports Show Minorities Lack Computers At Home," Houston Chronicle, October 31, 2003, p. 27.

Printed in the United States
136254LV00002B/7/A